Royal Horticultural Society

RHS GARDEN
PROBLEM
SOLVER

Royal Horticultural Society

RHS GARDEN PROBLEM SOLVER

MITCHELL BEAZLEY

RHS GARDEN PROBLEM SOLVER

First published in Great Britain in 2012 by Mitchell Beazley,
an imprint of Octopus Publishing Group Ltd, Endeavour House,
189 Shaftesbury Avenue, London WC2H 8JY
www.octopusbooks.co.uk

An Hachette UK Company
www.hachette.co.uk

Published in association with The Royal Horticultural Society.

Design and layout copyright © Octopus Publishing Group Ltd 2012
Text copyright © The Royal Horticultural Society 2012

ISBN: 978 1 84533 591 5

A CIP record for this book is available from the British Library.

Set in Gill Sans and Minion
Printed and bound in China

Author Rosemary Ward
Publishers Lorraine Dickey, Alison Starling
Commissioning Editor Helen Griffin
Senior Editor Leanne Bryan
Copy-editor Joanna Chisholm
Proofreader Jane Birch
Indexer Helen Snaith
Art Director Jonathan Christie
Senior Art Editor Juliette Norsworthy
Designer Lizzie Ballantyne
Picture Research Manager Giulia Hetherington
Senior Production Controller Caroline Alberti
RHS Commissioning Editor Rae Spencer-Jones
RHS Editor Simon Maughan
RHS Consultants Andrew Halstead and
  Beatrice Henricot

Note on pesticides
The term pesticide covers all
products used to kill pests of all
kinds. It includes insecticides,
fungicides, herbicides (weedkillers)
and molluscicides (slug and snail
killers). The ingredients, formulations
and brand names of pesticides can
vary from country to country, and
change frequently, so they are not
included in this book. All pesticides
used by gardeners must by law be
approved for specific garden uses,
and have the instructions needed to
apply them safely and effectively. It is
illegal to use home-made remedies
or products for professional use in
your garden. Approved products
have been thoroughly tested and
are safe when applied according to
the manufacturer's instructions.

CONTENTS

• INTRODUCTION •

At their best, gardens can be both productive and decorative, giving delight and satisfaction to the gardener, creating a practical and enjoyable space, and providing a haven for wildlife. Of course, difficulties will occur, but the purpose of this book is to help you to garden in ways that minimise problems, and to diagnose and deal effectively with those that do occur.

Understanding how environmental conditions affect plants, and how pests and diseases develop, are the initial keys to preventing many problems, and dealing effectively with those that do arise. It is the way to become a better gardener, and have even more success and enjoyment from your garden. Therefore, the first part of *RHS Garden Problem Solver* is dedicated to helping you understand your soil and climate and the most commonly occurring pests and diseases.

Once you have got to grips with how problems occur, you have a much better chance of preventing them – for example, by choosing the right plants, then giving them the best possible growing conditions. This means that your plants are less likely to succumb to problems in the first place, and if trouble

does strike they are in a better position to shake it off. Prevention also involves encouraging garden friends that will keep pest numbers down, and using clever gardening techniques to keep foes well away.

Despite your best efforts, plants can still respond badly to difficult growing conditions or suffer depredations from pests and infection by diseases. You will, therefore, find information on dealing with all the problems you are likely to encounter, whether these are with seed-raised plants, bulbs, glasshouse plants, herbaceous plants, lawns, trees or shrubs. This chapter includes tips on using cultural methods of control, as well as organic techniques and chemical controls. In addition, it tells you which problems you can afford to ignore. Similar information follows on vegetables and fruit, with a final chapter on dealing with weeds.

At the end of *RHS Garden Problem Solver* is a glossary of gardening terms.

Maintain a bountiful garden by understanding how problems occur and dealing with them effectively.

UNDERSTANDING PROBLEMS

• UNDERSTANDING ENVIRONMENTAL PROBLEMS •

Understanding the way that the weather, the soil and other elements of the environment affect plant growth will help spot and solve many common problems.

WATER

Plants without sufficient water will **wilt**. This starts as a protective mechanism by the plant, trying to reduce water loss from the undersides of the leaves by folding them down to reduce air movement. In later stages, the plant cells themselves lose firmness, and the soft parts of the plant collapse. Usually, this just means that the soil is too dry and if rewetted the plant should recover, provided it has not completely dried out.

Wilting can also occur in very hot or windy weather, when plant roots simply cannot keep up with water loss from the leaves. It may also mean that the roots have been damaged by waterlogging, or infection by root-rotting diseases, so always check before adding more water.

A fluctuating water supply, where soil or compost dries out between waterings, can lead to poor crops from susceptible plants such as cauliflower, celery and fennel. It can also result in fruit or root vegetables **splitting**.

TEMPERATURE

Plants vary greatly in their tolerance of different temperatures, and it is important to know their individual needs to grow them well. Damage by **frost** or **very cold winds** tends to be a problem in mid- to late spring, when new foliage appears on hardy plants and less hardy plants are moved outdoors. Unless plants are very small, or very badly affected, they usually recover.

Use fleece to protect vulnerable plants, such as tree ferns, over winter.

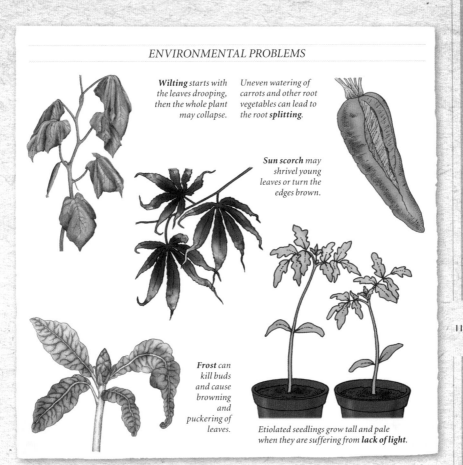

Wilting starts with the leaves drooping, then the whole plant may collapse.

Uneven watering of carrots and other root vegetables can lead to the root **splitting**.

Sun scorch may shrivel young leaves or turn the edges brown.

Frost can kill buds and cause browning and puckering of leaves.

Etiolated seedlings grow tall and pale when they are suffering from **lack of light**.

11

Sun scorch affects many golden and variegated plants, and others such as Japanese maples (*Acer japonicum*, *A. palmatum*) that have soft, delicate foliage. Sun scorch can also occur on plants grown under glass, causing general browning, and discoloured patches on fruit such as **greenback** on tomato (see p142).

LIGHT

Plants grown indoors often suffer from **too little light**, especially in winter, and may become drawn, pale and fail to flower. Move the plants to better light or replace with more shade-tolerant species. Seedlings quickly become drawn, or etiolated, in low light levels, especially when temperatures are high.

WIND

Gardens can suffer surprising amounts of **wind damage**. Broken branches and flattened plants are the obvious indications, but **scorching** of delicate leaves, lopsided development and a general reduction in growth also occur. Cold winds are a particular problem and can cause low-temperature damage, even in the absence of frost.

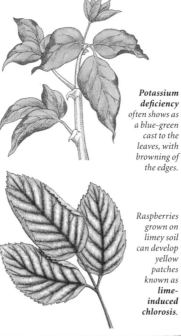

SOIL PROBLEMS

Potassium deficiency often shows as a blue-green cast to the leaves, with browning of the edges.

*Raspberries grown on limey soil can develop yellow patches known as **lime-induced chlorosis**.*

SOIL STRUCTURE

Below ground, the structure and constituents of the soil have just as much effect on a plant's growth as the weather above ground. The ideal soil has a good mixture of large and small particles with a high organic content. Such soil will retain nutrients and moisture without becoming waterlogged and will be easy for roots to penetrate.

SOIL PH

This measures how acid or alkaline the soil is and it is usually governed by the amount of lime that the soil contains. The complete pH scale goes from pH1 (the most acid) to pH14 (the most alkaline), but soils are usually within the range pH4–8. The centrepoint, pH7, is neutral, and most plants prefer to grow in pH6–7.5. Very wet, peaty soils and quick-draining, sandy ones both tend to be acid, because the lime is washed away. Soils that develop over granite or sandstone also tend to be acid. Acid soils are essential for growing those plants that cannot tolerate lime, such as rhododendrons, heathers (*Erica*) and blueberries, and most fruit prefers slightly acid soil. Otherwise, they may develop **lime-induced chlorosis**. Many clay soils are alkaline, as are soils

1. Sample the soil by taking a spoonful of soil from several places across the area you want to test. Mix them together well, then put a small amount into the test tube supplied in the soil test kit.

2. Add the correct amount of test solution as recommended in the instructions. Shake well to mix thoroughly and allow the soil to settle until you can clearly see the colour of the solution.

3. Find the pH by comparing the colour of the test solution with the chart provided in the kit. Note that larger gardens may require two or more separate tests from around the garden.

developing over chalk and limestone. Most vegetables and many garden plants prefer neutral or slightly alkaline soil. Check the pH of your soil with a test kit (see box above) from a garden centre.

SOIL MINERALS

A range of soil minerals is also essential for healthy plant growth. The most significant are those containing nitrogen (N), phosphorus (P) and potassium (K). These three are needed in the largest amounts, and are found in varying proportions in all general-purpose garden fertilisers. High-nitrogen fertilisers promote rapid growth and are invaluable to boost plants in spring and for greedy crops such as cabbage and potatoes. Phosphorus is particularly important for root growth, while potassium encourages the production of flowers and fruit and generally toughens plants up. Calcium, iron and magnesium are also needed in fairly large amounts, and sometimes have to be added to counteract specific deficiencies, but more often need adding when plants have problems in absorbing them from the soil. For example, lime-hating plants may need additional iron if the soil is not acid enough, and other plants can suffer from magnesium deficiency if there is too much potassium in the soil. Other minerals including boron, manganese and zinc are needed in tiny quantities and are collectively known as trace elements.

13

• UNDERSTANDING PESTS •

Plant pests can vary from large mammals such as deer and foxes to microscopic mites and nematodes. Identifying the culprit is the first essential step in dealing with a problem.

IDENTIFYING PESTS

If the pest is visible on the plant, then identification is relatively easy, though just because a creature is present it does not mean it is responsible for the damage. Often all you have to go on are symptoms, which help divide pests into broad groups: munchers and suckers.

MUNCHING PESTS

Munchers will generally be responsible when plants go missing altogether,

have missing parts, holes eaten in leaves and flowers or holes drilled into stems and roots. Large-scale destruction is likely to be caused by **deer**, **rabbits**, **badgers** or **birds** (see pp32–33), which will often leave other damage, or plant remains, in their wake. **Slugs** and **snails** (see p43) may be identified by slime trails, and **caterpillars** (see p41) by telltale droppings. Many pests such as **vine weevils** (see p44) or **earwigs** (see p73) prefer to feed under the cover of darkness, so search for them at night with a torch. Some pests such as slugs and snails will feed on almost any plants, whereas others such as **asparagus beetle** (see p112) are limited to a very few food plants, so can be easier to identify.

PLANT PESTS LARGE AND SMALL

*Some insect pests, such as **aphids**, are damaging both as juveniles and as adults.*

*Many damaging pests are the immature stages of harmless insects such as this **leatherjacket**, which is the larva of the crane fly or daddy-long-legs.*

Large pests may be less common, but can do considerable damage to plants.

PEST LIFE CYCLES

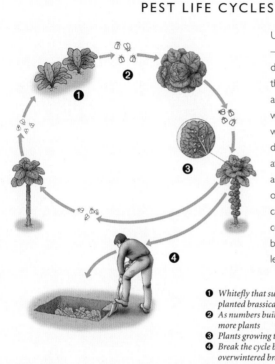

Understanding pest life cycles – both in terms of how they develop and how they live through the seasons – can be an invaluable tool when dealing with them. For example, brassica whitefly can be controlled by disposing of all infested foliage at the end of the season before any new brassicas are planted out. Pear midge numbers can be greatly reduced by collecting up affected fruitlets before the grubs are able to leave and pupate in the soil.

❶ *Whitefly that survive the winter move onto newly planted brassicas in spring*
❷ *As numbers build up, they spread out and affect more plants*
❸ *Plants growing through winter shelter the pests*
❹ *Break the cycle by burying or disposing of all overwintered brassicas before planting new ones*

SAP-SUCKING PESTS

These pests are all on the small side, and they attack plants by inserting a narrow feeding tube into a stem or leaf and extracting plant sap. In small numbers, the damage is insignificant, but large numbers can do substantial injury. Their telltale signs tend to be distorted plant growth, slight changes in leaf or stem colour, or browning. Many sap-sucking insects excrete honeydew as a waste product after having consumed so much sugary sap. This tends to attract **ants** (see p81), which collect it for their larvae, and **sooty mould** (see p90), which grows directly on the honeydew. Frequently, these signs of honeydew or sooty mould are more obvious than the pests that are causing the problem, and can help with diagnosis.

Plant diseases are predominantly caused by three types of organism: fungi, bacteria and viruses. Many, such as the periwinkle rust fungus or dahlia mosaic virus, affect only small groups of related plants. Others such as **honey fungus** (see p46) or **cucumber mosaic virus** (see p124) can attack a very wide range of species.

FUNGAL DISEASES

Powdery mildews, grey mould and other fungal diseases are generally spread by spores. Sometimes, these are produced by large, highly visible structures such as toadstools, but often they just appear as a powdery covering on affected plants, or as pinhead-sized fruiting bodies. The spores may be long-lived and some fungi can survive away from their host plants, sometimes for years. This is why fungal diseases such as **onion white rot** (see p130) are so difficult to eradicate from the soil.

The first symptom of some airborne fungal diseases is spots on leaves. These are usually round, distinctly coloured and sometimes with a halo of a different colour. Alternatively, there may be a powdery or velvety covering on affected leaves, stems, buds or flowers. Woody plants may have cankerous, dead, sunken areas surrounded by rough bark. Here the disease can overwinter to affect the leaves again in spring. Fungal diseases can often be discouraged by good hygiene and good cultivation. When they do strike, plants can often be saved with appropriate treatment.

DISEASE PROBLEMS

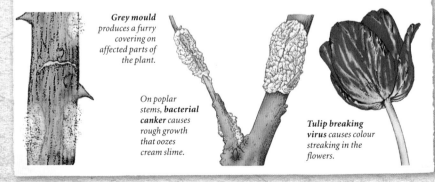

Grey mould produces a furry covering on affected parts of the plant.

On poplar stems, **bacterial canker** causes rough growth that oozes cream slime.

Tulip breaking virus causes colour streaking in the flowers.

DISEASE LIFE CYCLES

Many fungal diseases have quite complex life cycles that may even involve spending part of the year on different plants. Understanding how they reproduce and spread, and when, can be useful in working out how to control them. For example, rose blackspot can be reduced by removing leaves and shoots where spores overwinter, and mulching over spores on infected fallen leaves; peach leaf curl can be prevented by protecting plants from rain, which washes the spores into the opening buds.

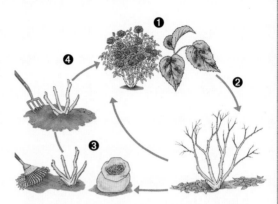

❶ Rose blackspot affects leaves and stems in spring and summer
❷ Spores overwinter on fallen leaves
❸ Spores reinfect the plant the following year
❹ Break the cycle by collecting fallen leaves, pruning out affected shoots and spreading mulch to cover up spores in fallen material

BACTERIAL DISEASES

Bacterial diseases such as **fireblight** (see p153) and **bacterial canker** (see p157) rarely live for long away from their host plant, and are usually spread by rain or wind or by direct contact on, say, unsterilized tools. They are often accompanied by oozing gum or slime or by large-scale die-back of branches. Bacterial infections may be fatal.

VIRAL DISEASES

Although there are many plant viruses, relatively few give serious cause for concern. **Virus** attacks may be symptomless, except for a general lack of vigour in a plant when compared with a virus-free one. At the other extreme, viruses can cause severe distortion, with extensive, yellow discoloration, and end up by killing the plant. Viruses rarely survive away from their hosts, and are usually spread by direct contact or by carriers known as vectors, which include **aphids** (see p40) and soil-dwelling nematodes. Viral diseases cannot be treated, though controlling the vectors can prevent infection.

• PREVENTING PROBLEMS •

To help minimise problems in your garden, there are two powerful strategies you can adopt. The first is to make positive choices to promote plant health. This means selecting good-quality plants that are suitable for your garden, and growing them well. The second strategy is to make it difficult for pests and diseases to reach your plants by practising good hygiene, using barriers and encouraging natural predators.

• CHOOSING THE RIGHT PLANTS •

Many plant problems can be avoided, or their impact reduced, by choosing the right plants in the first place. Plants that are in robust health when you buy them have a head start over specimens that are already struggling. Also, varieties chosen to suit the conditions you can provide will grow more strongly and be better able to cope with whatever weather conditions, pests or diseases occur.

BUYING HEALTHY PLANTS

Many plants offered for sale are not in tiptop condition, so it's useful to check proposed purchases carefully. Points to look for include:

- Healthy leaves with rich colours and no signs of yellowing in young or old leaves (indicating lack of food) or bronzing (indicating exposure to temperature extremes).

- No signs of damage, discolouration or distortion that may indicate pest or disease problems.

- A well-balanced shape – crucial for trees or slow-growing shrubs.

THE IDEAL PLANT

Reduce problems by choosing healthy plants of good varieties that will thrive in the conditions you can provide.

18

● Roots that just fill the pot, holding the compost together, but are not growing through the base or circling round inside the pot.

● Compost that is moist – not dry or waterlogged.

● No weeds on the surface of the compost (weeds can indicate a plant that has gone unsold for a long time).

● A proper label, with the full Latin name (so you can look up more about it) and basic care instructions.

● Plants that are not in full flower (unless you need to check the colour) as these will establish more readily.

● Where the plant is on sale: if it is growing outdoors, it can go straight into the garden; if it is under cover, the plant will need to be protected initially while it is hardened off before eventually being planted outdoors.

CERTIFIED PLANTS

For a few plants, there are certification schemes that guarantee a plant has been grown in conditions that greatly reduce the risk of it carrying pests and diseases. These schemes are run for the benefit of commercial growers, but are of value to amateur gardeners, too. Look out for certified apples, pears, cherries, plums, currants, raspberries, strawberries and seed potatoes.

RESISTANT VARIETIES

For many kinds of plants, you can reduce the risk of some pest and disease problems by looking for resistant varieties. These are most likely to be found among fruit and vegetables of commercial significance, such as apples and potatoes, or among plants that have large breeding programmes, such as bedding plants and roses. Throughout *RHS Garden Problem Solver* we have mentioned where pest- or disease-resistant varieties exist, though you should realise that even these varieties are rarely immune – they are just less likely to suffer.

TOLERANT VARIETIES

A few varieties are tolerant of aspects of the weather or particular soil problems. For example, you can find potatoes and tomatoes with some cold tolerance, golden-leaved plants with sun tolerance, and a strain of rhododendrons with greater-than-average lime tolerance.

• ESTABLISHING GOOD GROWING CONDITIONS •

PROVIDING FOOD AND WATER

Ensuring that plants have the conditions they need to grow well is the first step towards preventing problems.

Improving the soil

The best way to enhance soil quality is to incorporate lots of bulky organic material, such as well-rotted farmyard manure, garden compost, mushroom compost, spent hops or soil conditioner from a community composting scheme. This can be dug into the soil or spread on the surface for worms to work into the soil. Increasing the soil's organic content helps improve texture and drainage on heavy, clay soils, and moisture-holding and nutrient retention on light, sandy soils. Additional fertiliser is likely to be needed: for greedy crops such as potatoes and cabbages; on poor, sandy soils; where plant are grown at very close spacings; or where there are known deficiencies.

Where soil is the wrong pH for a plant (see p12), it is easy to make soil more alkaline by adding lime. It is much more difficult to make soil more acidic, so the best solution if you have alkaline soil is to grow lime-hating plants in tubs.

Plants in containers

A pot-grown plant needs good-quality compost that is appropriate to that type of plant. For example, seed and cutting compost has low fertiliser levels, whereas hanging basket composts include more fertiliser, as well as water-retaining granules. John Innes composts contain soil, which helps retain the structure of the compost for long-term plantings. After a few weeks in the same compost, most plants will need feeding with a controlled-release or liquid feed.

Watering

Water the soil, not the plant, and do so in the evening so less water evaporates. Water thoroughly once or twice a week in dry spells, not a little every day. Deeper containers are better than shallower ones as the soil dries out more slowly.

PROVIDING SHELTER

Additional shelter may protect plants from extreme weather and pests.

Windbreaks

Most plants grow better in a sheltered environment so windbreaks are a good investment in areas where strong winds are common. Solid walls or fences can create turbulence and trap cold air, creating a frost pocket, so the best windbreaks are semi-permeable.

Cold frames

These provide wind protection and will also retain the sun's heat, especially if fitted with glass. Cold frames are a useful half-way house in spring between a heated environment and outdoors.

Cloches

Plant covers – cloches – are useful for: warming the soil before planting; protecting tender, young plants; advancing cropping on plants such as French beans and strawberries; ripening crops such as onions and chillies at the end of summer; and protecting alpines from winter wet. Glass cloches can raise soil temperature by as much as 10°C (18°F) and advance cropping by up to four weeks; rigid plastic does this by three weeks. However, the humid atmosphere in a cloche can encourage disease, and the good growing conditions encourage rapid weed growth.

Tunnel cloches

These are similar but more economical than individual cloches. They can advance cropping by up to two weeks.

PLANT SHELTERS

Use hoops of wire, flexible willow or hazel wands, or plastic piping, covered with polythene or horticultural fleece, to create a **tunnel cloche**.

Windbreaks *such as hedges, porous walls and openwork fences are effective as they filter the wind without creating turbulence.*

A **cold frame** *consists of a wood or metal framework fitted with glass or rigid plastic panels.*

• USING GOOD GROWING TECHNIQUES •

The effects of some pests and diseases can be reduced by planting in certain combinations, or at specific times, or by treating plants in particular ways.

COMPANION PLANTING

One well-known, though largely unproven, technique is companion planting where one plant benefits another. This may be by improving its growth, as hyssop (*Hyssopus*) is supposed to enhance the development of grapes, or by discouraging pests: for example, marigolds (*Tagetes*) deterring whitefly from roses; onions disguising the carrot-fly-attracting aroma of carrots; and nasturtiums (*Tropaeolum*) attracting cabbage white butterflies away from brassicas.

A simpler variation is to plant vegetables in flower borders where pests are less likely to find them.

CLEVER TIMING

A more scientific technique is the use of clever timing to avoid damage. For example, early potatoes usually avoid **potato blight** (see p134), and digging maincrop potatoes as soon as they are ready greatly reduces **slug** damage (see p43). Sowing quick-maturing varieties of carrots as early as possible means

---

GROWING TECHNIQUES TO CONTROL PESTS

Interplanting cabbages and French beans may deter cabbage root fly and aphids.

Carrot flies finds their target by smell, so interplanting carrots with strong-smelling onions may put them off.

By the time broad beans flower, the tips are usually infested with blackfly, which can be removed by pinching out the tips.

FOUR-YEAR CROP ROTATION PLAN

	AREA 1	AREA 2	AREA 3	AREA 4
YEAR 1	**Potato family** aubergines, chillies, peppers, potatoes, tomatoes	**Roots and onions** beetroot, carrots, garlic, leeks, onions, parsnips	**Peas, beans and others** beans, courgettes, lettuces, peas, squash	**Brassicas** cabbages, cauliflowers, Chinese greens, kale, radishes, turnips
YEAR 2	**Brassicas**	**Potato family**	**Roots and onions**	**Peas, beans and others**
YEAR 3	**Peas, beans and others**	**Brassicas**	**Potato family**	**Roots and onions**
YEAR 4	**Roots and onions**	**Peas, beans and others**	**Brassicas**	**Potato family**

they can be harvested before the first **carrot flies** (see p120) are on the wing, while autumn-fruiting raspberries usually crop too late to be bothered by **raspberry beetle** (see p165).

PLANTING TECHNIQUES

Starting seeds off in pots often helps them to get ahead of the weather, but can also help to avoid, or reduce, some pest and disease problems. For example, **mice** and **voles** attack pea and bean seeds outdoors but not growing plants. Brassica seedlings grown in pots until they have a good root system are more likely to cope with attacks of **club root** (see p119).

CROP ROTATION

Adapted from the agricultural practice of moving crops and livestock from field to field, crop rotation is a useful weapon against attack by pests and disease. Crops are rotated for three main reasons: it reduces the build-up of soilborne pests and diseases; it makes efficient use of available nutrients in different levels of the soil; and it spreads different cultivation techniques across the whole plot. To operate crop rotation, vegetables are grouped in families, and each allocated a section of the plot (see box above). The following year each family moves to a different section.

• ENCOURAGING BENEFICIAL INSECTS •

There are two main groups of beneficial insects are far as gardeners are concerned: pollinators that ensure fruit and seed crops are fertilised, and predators that prey on pests.

To maintain a healthy population of these in your garden, keep insecticide use to a minimum, and target pests very carefully. Use insecticides only in the evening and never spray open flowers.

POLLINATORS

Honey bees are widely used, commercial pollinators in orchards. However, **bumble bees** are active earlier in the year, and in poorer weather, so can make all the difference to early bloomers such as pears. Also important are **mining bees**, which live in small burrows, and **mason bees**, which nest in gaps in

walls or similar spaces. Some **flies** are also good pollinators and are used to pollinate strawberries in tunnels.

The main way to attract pollinators is to ensure a succession of nectar-bearing flowers in your garden from spring to autumn. Examples include: pussy willow (*Salix caprea*), flowering currant (*Ribes sanguinea*) and hellebore (*Helleborus*) for spring; buddleia, lavender (*Lavandula*) and globe thistle (*Echinops*) for summer; sedum, Michaelmas daisy (*Aster novi-belgii*) and marjoram (*Origanum*) for autumn; ivy (*Hedera*) and erica for winter. Nest boxes have also been used successfully to attract mason bees.

PREDATORS

The rule of thumb for distinguishing friend from foe in the insect world is that friends move much more quickly because they are predators, whereas pests do not need much speed as they feed on plants. A good example is the speedy, carnivorous **centipede**,

Simple, open flowers like poached-egg plant (Limanthes) attract beneficial insects such as hoverflies.

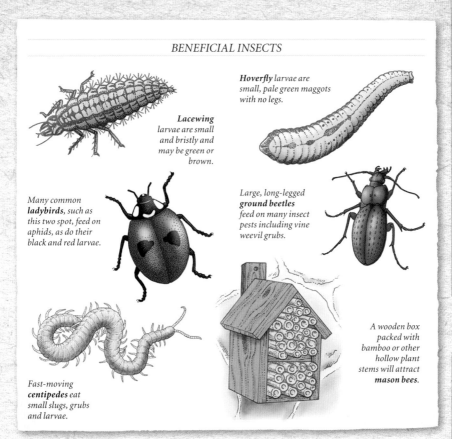

Hoverfly larvae are small, pale green maggots with no legs.

Lacewing larvae are small and bristly and may be green or brown.

Many common **ladybirds**, such as this two spot, feed on aphids, as do their black and red larvae.

Large, long-legged **ground beetles** feed on many insect pests including vine weevil grubs.

A wooden box packed with bamboo or other hollow plant stems will attract **mason bees**.

Fast-moving **centipedes** eat small slugs, grubs and larvae.

25

compared with the slow, vegetarian **millipede**. **Aphids** (see p40) are the food source for one particularly valuable group of insect predators – some **ladybirds** and their larvae, **hoverfly** larvae and **lacewing** larvae. Hoverfly and lacewing adults feed on pollen and nectar so will be interested in the same flowers as bees. The only way to attract ladybirds is to have aphids for them to feed on so try to leave some colonies where they are not doing much harm. You can buy ladybirds from suppliers of biological control, but as they can fly well they tend not to stay where you put them. Ground-dwelling predators such as centipedes and ground beetles like places to hide when not hunting, so organic mulches together with the odd log or pile of stones will attract them.

• ENCOURAGING WILDLIFE PREDATORS •

Larger wildlife – in particular, frogs and toads, insect-eating birds and hedgehogs – can be of great benefit to gardeners by feeding on plant pests. Frogs, toads and hedgehogs are widely credited with feasting on **slugs** and **snails** (see p43). In fact, they generally prefer beetles and worms, as do most birds, because slugs are just too slimy. However, there is no doubt they do eat some slugs, and probably hoover up various other pests such as **vine weevils** (see p44) and **wireworms** (see p136) in their nightly perambulations.

ATTRACTING BIRDS

*This type of **bird box** with a small entrance hole will attract insect-eating tits.*

BIRDS

Insectivorous birds, such as tits, robins and warblers, eat countless thousands of **caterpillars** (see p41), **greenfly** (see p40) and other pests throughout the year, and even seed-eating birds such as sparrows need insects to feed their young. Thrushes specialise in snails, although they are hard work and they will only take them when there isn't much other food about.

Most established gardens already provide a good supply of natural bird food in the form of insects, seeds and berries, and this can be supplemented with bird food that will bring in more birds and keep them for longer. If you can persuade birds to nest by providing suitable dense bushes, hollow trees, ivy-covered walls or appropriate bird boxes, then they will collect more pests to feed their families. Water is also essential for birds to drink and bathe, so a pond with shallow edges will attract them, too.

HEDGEHOGS

It is difficult to encourage hedgehogs; it is more a question of not discouraging them. They are likely to roam over

WILDLIFE POND

The ideal wildlife pond has deep areas for frogs to overwinter, and shallow edges for easy access. There should be a mixture of floating and submerged plants, and marginal ones rooted in the pond but growing out of it, as well as a boggy area.

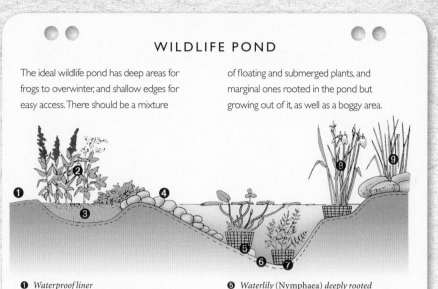

1. *Waterproof liner*
2. *Bog plants: purple loosestrife* (Lythrum salicaria) *and meadowsweet* (Filipendula ulmaria)
3. *Bog area filled with soil*
4. *Shallow slope with pebbles to cover the liner*
5. *Waterlily* (Nymphaea) *deeply rooted*
6. *Deep water for hibernating frogs*
7. *Submerged spiked water milfoil* (Myriophyllum spicatum)
8. *Marginal plant: water iris* (Iris laevigata)
9. *Long grass to provide cover and shade*

several gardens each night, so want easy access under fences, and need a sheltered hideaway where they can spend the winter. Do not leave loose netting about, which they can get tangled up in, and fit exit ramps in steep-sided ponds.

FROGS AND TOADS

These amphibians need water to breed, so a pond will always attract them, even though they spend most of the year on dry land. Provide some longer grass and other shady hiding places, such as log piles, for them to hide in.

DISTINGUISHING AMPHIBIANS

Frogs have moist, smooth skin, usually yellow or green with darker markings, and they hop more than they crawl.

Toads have dry, rough skin, usually grey-brown, and they crawl more than they hop.

• ESTABLISHING GOOD GARDEN HYGIENE •

The traditional advice regarding hygiene in the garden was pretty straightforward: surfaces were to be scrupulously scrubbed; dead, damaged, diseased or infested material burned; and all other plant debris tidied away and composted. Extraneous piles of leaves, wood or stone were not encouraged, and wildlife was, for the most part, thoroughly discouraged. The aim of all this cleaning and tidying was to make life as difficult as possible for pests and diseases to survive from one year to the next.

These days, the approach is much more relaxed. Few gardeners have the time to clean and clear all the time. They also want to encourage wildlife and understand the value of leafy hedge bottoms, wood piles, dead plant stems and other forms of 'untidiness' in helping it to survive. Consequently you have to strike a balance – practising good hygiene where it really matters, but leaving other areas a little rougher round the edges.

GLASSHOUSES

One area where good hygiene really does bring rewards is in the glasshouse. You can make a real difference to pest and disease problems by maintaining a good airflow, not allowing clutter to accumulate, clearing away any damaged plant material promptly, and giving the whole structure a thorough scrub once a year. Similarly, keeping pots, trays, tools and labels clean and using fresh water and fresh compost will make raising strong, healthy plants that bit easier.

GOOD HYGIENE TIPS

Picking off dead flowers and leaves promptly from glasshouse plants will reduce disease attacks.

Cutting off all the leaves from strawberries at the end of the season removes many disease spores as well. It helps birds searching for pests, too.

FRUIT AND VEGETABLE AREAS

In productive parts of the garden, maintain good hygiene as far as possible to prevent carry-over of pest and disease problems. For example, use inert materials to shelter ground beetles rather than rotting wood, and keep weeds well under control. Dispose of diseased plant material, or the seeds and storage roots of weeds, via a large-scale composting scheme, where the high temperatures reached will destroy disease organisms and weeds. If this option is not available, and burning not possible, then burying to more than a spade's depth is another alternative. At one time, fruit trees were routinely treated with tar-oil winter washes to kill overwintering pests.

Clean containers help you to grow healthier plants.

Unfortunately, this treatment also killed many overwintering predators and made some pests such as **fruit tree red spider mite** (see p42) worse, so is no longer recommended.

ORNAMENTAL AREAS

Unless you want to produce exhibition-standard blooms, or open your garden to the public, most hygiene rules can be more relaxed in the ornamental garden, where good planting for year-round interest will counteract any lack of tidiness or the odd bit of damage and allow wildlife to share your garden.

· BARRIERS FOR SMALL PESTS ·

The most effective way to deal with many pests, especially if you do not want to use pesticides, is to introduce barriers. The drawbacks are that they can be relatively expensive and can make access difficult. Some pest barriers such as cabbage collars have been around for a long time, while the idea of fine-mesh barriers against a wide range of insect pests is relatively new.

SOLID BARRIERS

Cabbage collars fit snugly round the stem to prevent **cabbage root fly** (see p118) reaching the base of a plant to lay its eggs. Other solid barriers include **copper rings**, which are designed to deter **slugs** and **snails** (see p43) by giving them a tiny electric shock, and **mini-cloches** cut from plastic bottles.

CARROT FLY BARRIERS

An interesting barrier idea involves the use of fleece, polythene sheeting or fine mesh held taut over a frame to deter **carrot flies** (see p120). These insects fly along close to the ground, locating carrots by scent. If they meet a barrier, they are either diverted sideways or fly up and over the top. However, they are weak fliers and cannot manoeuvre well enough to come straight down, so carrots within about 2m (6½ft) of a carrot-fly barrier are protected. The benefit of a barrier over a complete cover is that it allows in rain, does not crush the plants or allow them to overheat and enables you to have easier access for weeding and harvesting.

INSECT-PROOF TUNNELS

For most insects, a complete cover is necessary, and this usually takes the form of a **tunnel** supported on hoops. Early and late in the season the cover could be clear polythene or horticultural fleece, but in summer open mesh is better to allow in rain and ventilation.

SLUG-CONTROL BARRIER

*A clean **copper ring** with no leaves arching over to touch the ground will keep away slugs and snails.*

Ordinary, small-mesh netting (1cm/½in) will keep out butterflies and moths, but you will need a finer insect-proof mesh to exclude smaller pests. Standard grade will keep out most pests; and ultrafine grade will also exclude tiny insects such as **flea beetles** (see p111) and many **aphids** (see p40). Make sure the netting is well anchored all around, but easy to remove for access, and on hoops tall enough to remain clear of the crop all the time it is needed.

WHEN TO ERECT BARRIERS

The timing can be important when putting a barrier in position. The safest approach is just to keep the crop covered at all times, but this is impractical with tall crops. It also needs a lot of insect-proof mesh, and is often not necessary, so it is worth checking when your plants are most vulnerable. For example, sweet corn is prone to **frit flies** (see p139) only at the seedling stage; once the plant has seven leaves, the cover can be removed.

BARRIERS TO EXCLUDE SMALL PESTS

A home-made **mini-cloche** keeps cold draughts and many pests away from vulnerable young plants.

A **cabbage collar** is a 15cm (6in) square of thick material such as carpet underlay.

A **carrot fly barrier** is a rigid frame, 75cm (30in) high, surrounded by polythene sheeting, horticultural fleece or fine-mesh netting.

Fine-mesh netting tunnels protect plants from flying pests. Fine net curtains are a cut-price alternative.

• BARRIERS FOR LARGE PESTS •

Deterrent devices, repellent chemicals or plants to deter larger foes are very rarely effective for more than a short period, especially if there is little natural food on offer. Barriers are generally the only effective way to protect plants from being disturbed or eaten by badgers, birds, cats, deer, foxes, rabbits or squirrels.

BADGERS

One of the biggest problems with badgers is that they excavate lawns, often in search of **chafer grubs** (see p80), so controlling these may solve the problem. However, badgers will also dig up root vegetables and are particularly fond of sweet corn. Ordinary fencing will not deter them, so use electric fences, turning them on at night.

BIRDS

Fruit-eating birds will attack most kinds of fruit; bullfinches and some other species will eat fruit buds in winter; pigeons will strip brassica plants; and jays are particularly fond of peas. Use netting to keep all these birds at bay: 2.5cm (1in) mesh will protect fruit crops and fruit buds from small birds; while 10cm (4in) mesh will keep pigeons off brassicas, and jays off peas, provided they cannot peck at the crops through the mesh. For short-term protection, low-level structures can work well. For permanent protection, a fruit cage gives much easier access for the gardener.

DEER

These animals are expanding in range and numbers and are an increasing

---

BARRIERS TO EXCLUDE LARGE PESTS

*Flowerpots on bamboo canes help support a **net** to protect black currant buds from birds.*

Netting should be stretched tight so wildlife does not become entangled.

Rabbit-proof fencing should be at least 75cm (30in) high, with 15cm (6in) turned out at the base and buried.

Small-mesh netting is the best way to protect brassicas from cabbage white butterflies, and will also deter pigeons.

menace in gardens. Deer eat everything from runner beans to roses, and also damage trees by eating or scraping off strips of bark. The only sure protection is fencing, which needs to be 1.5m (5ft) high for smaller deer and 2m (6½ft) or more for larger ones.

FOXES

Damage associated with foxes includes their digging for worms and grubs and breaking spurs from fruit trees when feeding on apples and pears. Young cubs can also flatten plants while playing. Protect individual plants, or small areas of the garden, with cages. Fencing the garden is largely ineffective as foxes can burrow – and climb, like cats.

RABBITS

Rabbit tastes are rather unpredictable. Experimentation and local knowledge should provide a good range of ornamental plants they will avoid, but vegetables will have to be fenced using 2.5cm (1in) square or 3cm (1⅛in) hexagonal wire mesh. Fit tree trunks with tree guards, to protect the bark.

SQUIRRELS

The main damage caused by squirrels in gardens is taking bulbs, nuts, fruit and seeds such as sweet corn, though they can also attack tree bark. Protect bulbs by covering with wire netting. Cages for fruit or nuts may also need to be wire, as squirrels can easily chew through plastic.

• STICKY TRAPS •

Trapping insects with sticky materials has been used for a long time as a way to protect fruit trees, and is now used for a wider range of pests. Traps may consist of: sticky bands fixed in the path of crawling insects; sticky hanging cards that attract by colour; or partly enclosed traps that attract by scent.

STICKY BANDS

Female **winter moths** (see p147) have only rudimentary wings, so must crawl up fruit tree trunks to lay their eggs on the leaf buds. Bands of grease or other sticky substances around the trunk will trap the moths and protect the leaves from **caterpillar** damage (see p41). **Vine weevils** (see p44) are also unable to fly, so sticky bands around pots can prevent them reaching the compost to lay eggs. Keep sticky bands free of dirt and debris to remain effective, and replace them at least once a year.

COLOURED TRAPS

Sticky traps can also be used to catch flying insects. Initially, these traps were developed to monitor insect

---

INSECT TRAPS

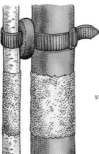

Apply **sticky bands** above the level of surrounding vegetation. If the tree has a stake, either put the band above the tie, or grease the stake as well.

Coloured sticky traps are covered with non-drying glue and catch insects indiscriminately.

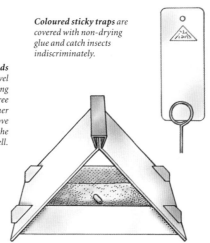

Pheromone traps contain a baited lure to attract male moths.

populations in a particular crop and help time the use of sprays or biological controls more effectively. Gardeners have found that using the traps alone can reduce pest numbers significantly. Yellow sticky traps attract a wide range of insects, but are mostly used in glasshouses to lure **whitefly** (see p44). Blue sticky traps attract **thrips** (see p61), and catch fewer harmless insects than

Timing is important with pheromone traps, so check this before you erect one.

yellow traps. Replace the traps when the surface becomes covered with insects.

PHEROMONE TRAPS

Some sticky traps use the insect's own communication system to trap them. Female moths produce scented chemicals called pheromones, which attract males. Lures are impregnated with synthetic copies of the pheromone, then placed on a sticky sheet inside a weather-proof trap. The males are attracted by the scent and trapped on the sticky sheet, so fewer females are fertilised and fewer viable eggs laid. These traps are available for **codling moth** (see p151), **plum moth** (see p155) and **pea moth** (see p133). It's important to check the instructions and hang them at the right time of year. New lures will be needed each season.

USING PESTICIDES PREVENTIVELY

Preventive spraying for both pest and disease control used to be routine in many areas of the garden, especially for roses and fruit. This is no longer recommended for several reasons: most people aim to reduce pesticide use where possible; spraying may be unnecessary, wasting time and money; pests can build up resistance to pesticides and will do so more quickly the more they are used; many harmless organisms can be unintentionally damaged by routine spraying.

That said, preventive spraying still has a place where problems are known to occur regularly, especially where these are difficult to control once established. Examples are given where appropriate in the chapters on solving problems.

TAKING
ACTION

• IMPROVING GROWING CONDITIONS •

If plants are not thriving, you can help them to recover by improving their growing conditions, even if you know they are suffering from a particular pest or disease.

WATER

Aim to water plants before they get to the stage of **wilting** (see p10) – look for more subtle signs of stress such as slow growth and dull foliage. Water thoroughly and repeat daily until the plant recovers. Mulch where practical to retain soil moisture. If watering is needed regularly, consider fitting an irrigation system using drip-feeding nozzles or porous pipe that will release water slowly directly to the base of the plant, so none is wasted. If compost in pots becomes very dry, it can shrink from the sides of the pots and be difficult to rewet, so water just drains through. Either immerse the pot in a bucket of water until air stops bubbling out, or stand the pots in a deep tray of water in a cool place for several hours.

NUTRIENTS

Plants short of food grow slowly, with dull, yellow or bronzy leaves and reduced flowering and fruiting. Aim to build up soil fertility long term with organic matter but in the short term granular fertilisers, such as growmore or pelleted chicken manure, will give a quick boost. Applying liquid feed directly onto the leaves with a sprayer can also be effective. Most

An irrigation system makes it easier to provide a steady moisture supply.

Water in early morning or late afternoon, and direct the water around the base of the plant.

Granular fertiliser may be organic or inorganic and is easily applied to boost growing crops.

After frost or wind damage, a double layer of horticultural fleece provides a temporary shelter.

general fertilisers contain only the basic nutrients – nitrogen, phosphorus and potassium (see p13). If you identify a deficiency of iron or magnesium, there are specific products to deal with these: chelated or sequestered iron and Epsom salts or magnesium sulphate. Otherwise, look for a broad-based fertiliser that also contains minor elements.

LIGHT

House plants should be chosen to suit the amount of light available, but supplementary lighting can be useful to boost young plants indoors. The human eye adapts very well to low light and gives an inaccurate impression of light levels. Use a light meter for a truer reading. Fluorescent tubes are suitable for lighting plants, but need to be positioned near them as they emit only low levels of light. Metal halide lamps are better. The ideal is a mix of metal halide, sodium and mercury lamps to provide the full spectrum of light that plants require.

SHELTER

Plants that have suffered from **frost** (see p10) or **wind** damage (see p12) can be helped to recuperate with a temporary shelter. Slightly porous materials such as horticultural fleece, are best, to allow some air flow and prevent condensation, which can encourage rotting. Once the plant perks up, remove the shelter.

Control pests only where they are likely to do significant damage. Many are important parts of natural ecosystems: for example, recycling dead plant material or providing food for birds. The next few pages look at the options for controlling ten widely occurring pests.

APHIDS

These insects live in groups and feed by sucking sap from stems, leaves, flower buds or roots. Once feeding, they tend to stay put, though winged individuals do appear, and some species migrate between two types of plant for different periods of the year. Aphids reproduce very rapidly, so the sooner you take action the less plant damage will occur. Squash small numbers or remove them by nipping off badly infested shoots. Brush off black, shiny aphid eggs overwintering on bark, or spray them with a winter wash. Aphids have many natural predators (see p24), which should be encouraged. In glasshouses, biological control by a predatory midge (*Aphidoletes*) or a parasitic wasp (*Aphidius*) can be introduced. Contact insecticides may be used, but systemic insecticides are more effective, especially for leaf-curling aphids.

CAPSID BUGS

Sap-sucking capsid bugs move around as individuals feeding on leaves and buds, but by the time the damage is noticed the capsid bug is often long gone. This makes these pests difficult

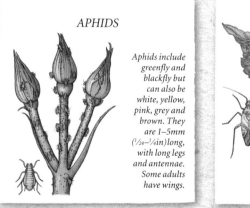

APHIDS

Aphids include greenfly and blackfly but can also be white, yellow, pink, grey and brown. They are 1–5mm ($\frac{1}{24}$–$\frac{1}{4}$in) long, with long legs and antennae. Some adults have wings.

CAPSID BUGS

Capsid bugs may be pale yellow, green or red-brown. They grow to 6mm ($\frac{1}{4}$in) long and have long legs and antennae. Adults have wings.

to control, but keeping down the weeds that they also feed on will help. If plants have been significantly injured in the past, check them from time to time and use an appropriate insecticide as soon as any further damage occurs.

CATERPILLARS

Among the most damaging caterpillars are those of the large white and small white butterflies, known as cabbage whites. All other problematic caterpillars belong to moths. Exclude butterflies and moths from crops by using insect-proof mesh. Squash eggs and small caterpillars, and pick off larger ones. Some insecticides are effective against young caterpillars, but less so against older ones. There is also a biological control using the nematode *Steinernema carpocapsae*, which is particularly useful on edible crops where insecticide use is limited.

LEAF MINERS

Some small flies and small moths have leaf-mining larvae. On trees, control is often not needed and rarely practical – though collecting and burning leaves at the end of the season will reduce numbers on isolated specimens. On most ornamental plants, leaf miners do little real damage, but mines may look unsightly. Squashing the miners or picking off affected leaves may help. With vegetables, exclude the adults using insect-proof mesh. Crop rotation (see p23) also helps keep numbers down, and some insecticides are approved for use on beet miner.

41

CATERPILLARS

Caterpillars have three pairs of legs at the front and up to five pairs of fleshy prolegs at the back.

LEAF MINERS

Leaf miners tunnel between the upper and lower leaf surfaces, producing characteristic linear or blotchy mines.

RED SPIDER MITES

Although barely visible individually to the naked eye, being around 1mm (¹⁄₂₄in) long, red spider mites can build up to huge numbers in warm, dry conditions, when they are easier to spot. Search any mottled foliage and wispy webs. There are several species, some of which are a particular problem in glasshouses. Others species feed on fruit trees or conifers. Red spider mites can be controlled using the predatory mite *Phytoseiulus persimilis*, but it must be introduced before pest levels build up too high. This predatory mite works well in glasshouses and can also be successful outdoors in hot summers. The alternative is to apply a suitable pesticide; several applications are likely to be needed, especially for those acting only on contact.

SAWFLIES

Adult sawflies are inconspicuous insects, similar to flying ants, and they feed mainly on pollen. The larvae look very like **caterpillars** (see p41). Many larvae feed together on leaves and can cause extensive damage. Other species graze the leaf surface, sometimes in a rolled-up leaf, or burrow into fruit. It is not practical to control sawfly larvae on trees, but birds will help to reduce numbers. On shrubs and herbaceous plants, pick off the pests or spray with a suitable contact or systemic insecticide.

SCALE INSECTS

These sap-sucking insects, 1–13mm (¹⁄₂₄–¹⁄₂in) long, may be white, green, grey, brown or black. They live on stems and the undersides of leathery leaves and

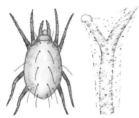

RED SPIDER MITES

Glasshouse red spider mites are only red over winter; normally, they are pale and hard to spot.

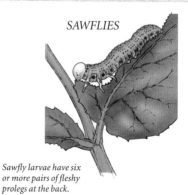

SAWFLIES

Sawfly larvae have six or more pairs of fleshy prolegs at the back.

can be very inconspicuous until they lay their eggs, which may be contained in white egg sacs. The other sign is black **sooty mould** (see p90) growing on the honeydew that some scale insects excrete. Immature scale insects, known as crawlers, are mobile but adults cannot move, so brushing or scraping off scales is an effective control. The crawlers are susceptible to insecticides so check once egg masses are spotted and spray when they hatch out. Otherwise, systemic insecticides will help control adults.

SLUGS AND SNAILS

It is not possible to clear the garden of slugs and snails, so the aim must be to control numbers in the areas they do most damage. Reducing the places near vulnerable plants where they can hide by day will help, as slugs and snails prefer not to travel far. Hand picking will also have some impact. Copper rings, tape or mesh create an effective barrier. Metaldehyde slug pellets are very effective, but are toxic to pets and wildlife if eaten. A liquid version can be watered in to kill slugs in the soil. Pellets based on ferric phosphate also work very well, are less harmful to other creatures, and can be used by organic gardeners. Another approach is to water on the biological control nematode *Phasmarhabditis hermaphrodita*, which is effective against slugs and young snails, though it can give disappointing results in heavy, clay soils. Spring and autumn are the best times to use it – the nematodes working best when the soil temperature is 5–20°C (41–68°F).

43

SCALE INSECTS

Adult scale insects are protected by a hard or waxy covering, usually green or brown.

SLUGS AND SNAILS

Slugs and snails come in a range of shapes and sizes and will feed on the soft parts of plants.

VINE WEEVIL

Adult vine weevils cannot fly, but are surprisingly mobile. They feed at night, mostly on shrubs, so can be caught and killed by torchlight, or may be found hiding under debris or pot plants by day. Apply insect barrier glue around containers to trap adults before they reach the compost to lay eggs. Young vine weevil grubs are susceptible to some systemic insecticides, but older ones are virtually immune. Insecticides can be applied as a soil drench to ornamental plants in containers, but cannot be used in open ground or on edible plants. There is also a biological control nematode, *Steinernema krausii*, which is best applied in late summer or early autumn and remains active down to 5°C (41°F). It is most effective in pots, and gives variable results in open ground, especially in heavy, clay soils.

WHITEFLY

Whitefly are sap-feeders, and the adults rise up in clouds when disturbed. There are several species, the most damaging of which attacks glasshouse plants. Others feed on brassicas, and a number of shrubs. In glasshouses, use yellow sticky traps to stop numbers building up. Small populations can also be controlled using a tiny parasitic wasp, *Encarsia formosa*. Indoors or out, insecticides will kill adults and scales, but eggs and pupae are immune so repeated spraying will be needed. Some whitefly populations are resistant to the most effective pesticides, so you may need to try different ingredients.

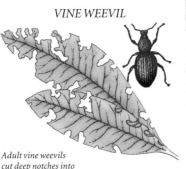

VINE WEEVIL

Adult vine weevils cut deep notches into leathery leaves. The grubs damage roots.

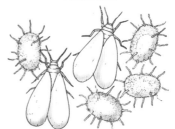

WHITEFLY

Whitefly are pure white, up to 2mm (1/12in) long, with immobile, scale-like larvae.

• COMMON DISEASES •

Many diseases are specific to small groups of plants, so control can be limited to the affected plants. With others, such as honey fungus and grey mould, any plant in the vicinity could be at risk, so all need to be considered.

DOWNY MILDEWS

Young plants and soft foliage are the main targets for downy mildews, which can develop quickly and kill vulnerable plants. Specific downy mildews are a significant problem on some vegetables including lettuce, onion and spinach, and some bedding plants including impatiens and pansy (*Viola × wittrockiana*). Good hygiene (see p28) is the first step to controlling them, keeping good air circulation and removing dead or damaged foliage promptly. Crop rotation (see p23) will reduce the build-up of spores. There are no chemical controls available for amateur gardeners.

GREY MOULD

Perhaps the commonest of all garden fungi is grey mould or botrytis, which affects anything and everything where conditions are right – a weak or damaged plant and a still, damp atmosphere. Good hygiene (see p28) is the best defence, removing dead material even before the rot sets in, coupled with good ventilation. Using garden disinfectant, thoroughly clean a glasshouse and equipment where grey mould has been prevalent. There are no chemical controls for amateur gardeners.

DOWNY MILDEW

Downy mildews tend to produce soft-looking, mouldy patches on foliage.

GREY MOULD

Grey mould is encouraged by high humidity to produce grey, velvety fungal growth.

HONEY FUNGUS

Almost all woody perennial plants, including rhubarb, can be affected by honey fungus, though susceptibility varies greatly from one genus to another. The fungus can survive on dead stumps and woody debris, and spreads underground though fine, black, root-like rhizomorphs. The first symptoms are usually sudden die-back or early leaf fall over the whole plant. Peeling back the bark at the base reveals a thin layer of white fungal growth, the texture of mushroom skin, with a strong, mushroomy smell. Once established, honey fungus is almost always fatal. There is no chemical treatment, but removal of all affected plants, together with as much of the root system as possible and woody debris in the ground, will starve out honey fungus. Vertical barriers, erected 30cm (12in) below ground (45cm/18in on very open soils) and 15cm (6in) above, can stop rhizomorphs spreading from infected plants or stumps that cannot be removed. In a hedge, also dig up and destroy healthy plants from 1m (3ft) either side of the infected ones.

LEAF SPOTS

Many fungal infections produce leaf spots. Often they have little or no effect on a plant's overall health, though they may appear unsightly. If more severe, they can cause reduced growth, premature leaf fall and, on woody plants, the disease may kill areas of stem to produce cankers. Plants that are growing well are less likely to succumb

HONEY FUNGUS

A white, fungal layer under the bark indicates honey fungus. Pale brown toadstools may also appear.

LEAF SPOTS

Leaf spots may be dark or pale, often with a distinct border or halo.

46

to leaf spots, so providing good growing conditions (see p20) is the first line of defence. If only a few leaves are affected, pick them off. Also clear up any fallen leaves or crop remains at the end of the season, because many leaf spot fungi overwinter on plant debris (see p17). Some leaf spots are susceptible to fungicides, as detailed in later chapters, though several applications are likely to be needed to achieve control.

PHYTOPHTHORA

Most plants can be affected by root diseases caused by phytophthora, though susceptibility varies a great deal. There are several species of this fungus-like organism, and they are responsible for many plant deaths in gardens. They tend to be worse in wet conditions such as poorly drained soils or long periods of wet weather. Once a plant is infected it will not recover, so prevention is the only remedy. In wet soils, plant on a small mound and do not overuse organic mulches. Remove dead plants promptly, together with all the soil around the roots. This can safely be used under a lawn, or to grow annual plants, including vegetables.

POWDERY MILDEWS

A very wide range of plants can be affected by powdery mildews, even though each type of mildew affects only a small group of plants. They spread mostly by windborne spores, and are worst in warm, dry conditions, especially when plants are short of moisture. Keeping plants well watered

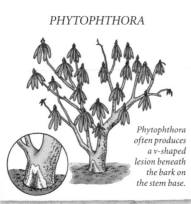

PHYTOPHTHORA

Phytophthora often produces a v-shaped lesion beneath the bark on the stem base.

POWDERY MILDEWS

Powdery mildews generally form a grey or white coating and may cause distortion.

(see p38) is, therefore, an important line of defence. If caught early, mildews can be controlled by fungicides, but badly affected leaves are best removed. Preventive spraying can be worthwhile on very susceptible plants, such as some roses and apples. Improving ventilation by pruning crowded stems and branches can help. Remove all plant debris at the end of the season and prune out affected shoots on shrubs and small trees. Choose resistant varieties of, for example, apples, gooseberries, peas and Michaelmas daisies (*Aster novi-belgii*).

RUSTS

Many plants are susceptible to specific rust diseases. The rust fungi have very complex life cycles, often producing spores of various colours, and living on alternative plants, at different stages. Rusts can spread very quickly, especially on soft foliage, so do not apply too much nitrogen fertiliser. Pick off any affected leaves as soon as they are seen. Rusts can lead to early leaf fall but, overall, do not seem to do a lot of damage to affected plants. Fungicides may be used to treat rust, and there are resistant varieties of, for example, antirrhinum, chrysanthemum and rose.

SCLEROTINIA

This disease tends to attack stem bases, or storage organs such as bulbs and swollen roots. Affected parts rot, and leaves above the damage turn yellow and die. The main control challenge is the long-lived sclerotia, which can live in the soil for many years. Carefully remove

RUSTS

Rust diseases normally show on the leaf surface as small, yellow spots, and underneath as darker, powdery masses, often orange, brown or black.

SCLEROTINIA

Plant stems affected by sclerotinia diseases usually develop a whitish mould containing black resting bodies called sclerotia.

diseased plants, together with soil in the immediate vicinity. There is no chemical treatment available to amateur gardeners, although professionally applied soil sterilants can be effective.

VERTICILLIUM WILT

Plants that wilt suddenly on one side may be affected by verticillium wilt. This soil-living disease enters through the roots, then moves up into the rest of the plant. Many types of plant can be affected, but it is most often noticed in trees and shrubs. Brown staining appears under the bark. Sometimes the application of an ammonium-based fertiliser can help the plant to overcome the disease. Disinfect tools after pruning. Remove dead plants with as much root as possible. Rotate vegetable crops (see p23), and replace trees and shrubs with less susceptible species.

VIRUSES

These minute organisms rarely live for long away from their hosts. They may be spread by contact or, more often, by carriers including **aphids** (see p40) and soil-dwelling nematodes. Many plants can tolerate low levels of viral infection with no obvious symptoms except rather lack-lustre performance that could have many other causes. Viruses cannot be treated, so remove plants with more definite symptoms, disinfect tools and wash your hands before working on other plants. Avoid viral problems by controlling aphid carriers and choosing resistant varieties of, for example, potatoes and raspberries.

49

VERTICILLIUM WILT

Verticillium wilt attacks a number of woody plants, causing die-back often on only one side. Dark streaks appear in the wood.

VIRUSES

Viruses can produce many symptoms, or none at all, but typically include yellow patterns, or blotches, and distorted growth.

ORNAMENTALS

• INTRODUCTION •

Problems that can arise on plants grown for decoration include an extensive range of pests and diseases as well as problems caused by the environment in which the plants are growing. In this chapter, plants are arranged in broad groups according to how they are grown, because this also reflects the types of pests and diseases they are likely to be affected by. Having looked at what can go wrong with seeds and seedlings in general, any problems specific to annuals and bedding plants, bulbs or corms, plants grown in a glasshouses, herbaceous border plants and lawns are described. Trees and shrubs vary enormously in their tolerance of pests and diseases, while roses are considerably more vulnerable to attack.

• SEEDS & SEEDLINGS •

SOLVING SEED PROBLEMS

Seeds are resistant to most plant diseases. Flower seeds are generally too small to attract pests, but **mice** or **birds** may take larger seeds, such as sweet peas

Good growing conditions give vulnerable seedlings the best chance to thrive.

(*Lathyrus odoratus*), so start them off in pots covered with fine wire netting.

If seeds **fail to germinate**, they may just be too old or of poor quality. Otherwise, lack of warmth, moisture or air may be the problem. Always use good-quality compost or well-cultivated soil for seed sowing as this will help achieve a good balance of air and moisture. If seeds rot, the growing medium is too wet. All seeds need a minimum temperature to germinate, according to species, and this can vary from about 5°C (41°F) for hardy plants to as much as 20°C (68°F) for some exotics. Always check before you start that enough heat is available.

SOLVING SEEDLING PROBLEMS

Seedlings growing indoors are most likely to suffer from too little light or from diseases encouraged by high humidity. Where seedlings become **etiolated** (pale and drawn) they are getting too much heat for the available light, so reduce the temperature. Seedlings that develop **downy mildew** should be disposed of as soon as possible. Do not compost them Ideally burn them or bury them deeper than 50cm (20in). When seedlings keel over at soil level, this is due to **damping off**. Remove affected seedlings and spray the remainder with a copper-based fungicide. Water only with clean, fresh supplies and improve ventilation.

53

Severe cold can scorch seedlings growing outdoors, or produce colour changes such as bronzing, yellowing or turning white. Cover seedlings damaged by cold, **heavy rain** or **drying winds** with cloches.

Seedlings that have been cut off at or below ground level have probably been attacked by **cutworms** (see p55) – moth caterpillars that live in the soil and emerge to feed at night. Check the soil near damaged seedlings to see if you can find the culprit. If seedlings have holes in the leaves or have disappeared altogether, suspect **slugs** (see p43).

54

Annuals and bedding plants are particularly vulnerable in the early stages, when weather can wreak havoc with new growth, and pests and diseases take advantage of underdeveloped roots and soft, defenceless leaves and stems. Providing good growing conditions to reduce stress on the young plants will help them avoid problems, and any that do arise will need prompt action to prevent serious damage.

ENVIRONMENTAL PROBLEMS

Frost, **wind** or **high temperatures** can kill annuals and bedding plants that have been grown under cover and not been properly prepared for the move outdoors. If damage is not too severe,

Seed-raised plants are less vulnerable to problems once fully grown.

protect affected plants with: glass or plastic for warmth; fine netting or horticultural fleece for shade; and any of these for shelter. To avoid problems, harden plants off by putting them out for part of the day only, then bringing them in again, for about a week before planting out.

SHOOT-EATING PESTS

Slugs and **snails** are likely to cause most trouble. You may detect their telltale, silvery slime trails where plants have been eaten. Slugs and snails are difficult to control but you can reduce their numbers in specific areas by collecting them up at night, or drowning them in traps consisting of a sunken container filled with beer or other sweet liquid. There are effective chemicals for slug control, but these should be used with care as some could poison pets or wildlife. Parasitic nematodes can be watered on but, to be effective, the soil needs to be moist and warm (see p43).

Damage to stems, leaves and flowers can also be caused by **caterpillars** (see p41), which you should remove, though you may need to do this after dark as many are night feeders. Damage can also be caused by **earwigs** (see p73) which also feed mainly at night. Spray with an appropriate insecticide as necessary.

Damage at or below soil level could be caused by **cutworms**. These nibble the roots and base of the stems, causing young plants to collapse and older plants to wilt or grow poorly. You may find them if you poke around just below the surface near damaged plants. There are no chemical controls available.

SAP-SUCKING PESTS

Aphids, a large group of insects including various greenfly and blackfly, feed by sucking sap from plants. In large numbers, they can weaken the plant

PESTS OF SEED-RAISED PLANTS

Cutworms *are dirty white, greyish or brownish caterpillars, to 4cm (1½in) long. They are larvae of various moths including the large and the lesser yellow underwing moth and the turnip moth.*

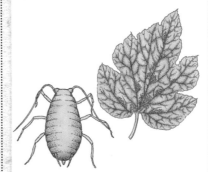

Aphids *appear in clusters at shoot tips and underneath leaves. They are 1–2mm (¹⁄₂₄–¹⁄₁₂in) long, with or without wings, and may be green, black, brown or grey.*

55

and, as they often cluster on shoot tips, they can seriously distort new growth. Aphids also spread viral diseases so it is important to control them where viruses are a problem, such as on sweet peas (*Lathyrus odoratus*). Squash small numbers by hand; otherwise, use a suitable systemic or contact insecticide.

DISEASE PROBLEMS

Many plant diseases are specific to particular plant groups so, for example, **pansy downy mildew** affects only pansies (*Viola* × *wittrockiana*) and violas. Other types of plant should remain healthy; and if plants die you can replant in the same place, provided you choose something unrelated. The drawback is that once the disease gets a hold it can sweep through all similar plants, which can be particularly devastating to displays of bedding.

Because bedding plants are short-lived, often the most practical approach to disease problems is to remove affected plants, improve the growing conditions where necessary, and replant with something different. However, early identification and treatment can reduce the spread of disease and may help save affected individuals.

DISEASES OF SEED-RAISED PLANTS

Pansy downy mildew starts off as purple-brown spots with fluffy growth underneath. In a bad attack, the leaves turn yellow and the whole plant may die.

Antirrhinum rust produces dark brown spore clusters on the undersides of leaves.

Aster wilt begins with the base of the stem becoming black and pinched, then the whole plant collapses.

Sweet peas can suffer from a range of **viruses**. Affected plants become distorted and show yellow specks and streaks.

SPOTS ON LEAVES

Fungal leaf spot diseases create small, circular areas of discoloration that gradually enlarge and may join up to form blotches. Removing affected leaves, then spraying with a suitable fungicide, may bring them under control. Leaf spots can also occur on plants under stress so providing good growing conditions will help to avoid them.

Rust diseases often start off looking like leaf spots, but then the fungus produces a mass of powdery spores – usually white, yellow, orange, brown or black – on leaf undersides. Rusts are rarely fatal. Remove the worst affected leaves, including any that have fallen, and treat the plants with a suitable fungicide. **Pansy rust** distorts stems; remove affected plants. Other bedding plants that commonly suffer rust problems include antirrhinums, double daisies (*Bellis*), hollyhocks (*Alcea*) and sweet Williams (*Dianthus barbatus*).

MOULDY OR DISTORTED LEAF PROBLEMS

A white, powdery coating, often accompanied by some distortion and generally poor growth, points to **powdery mildew** (see p47). There are hundreds of types, each affecting particular plants but the conditions that encourage them are similar. Powdery mildew attacks plants that are overcrowded, or stressed by lack of moisture in the soil, so thinning out and watering can help stave it off. If caught early, spraying with an appropriate fungicide can help; bad attacks are often fatal.

Viruses usually appear as yellow flecks and streaks, accompanied by distorted leaves and flowers. Sweet peas are particularly prone. As viruses cannot be treated, destroy affected plants.

Discoloured leaves that develop mouldy patches, which then disintegrate, have probably been attacked by **downy mildew**. This spreads rapidly in damp conditions, especially among crowded plants. Affected plants can be killed in a few days. Susceptible plants include *Nicotiana* and pansy.

STEM AND ROOT PROBLEMS

If plants suddenly collapse, or some of the shoots in a clump die back, check if there is evidence of physical damage or dry soil. If not, then suspect rotting by fungi. **Aster wilt** and **pansy sickness** are typical of these fungi, and they tend to destroy the base of a stem or the top of a root. It's generally best to cut your losses and remove the plants.

• BULBS & CORMS •

Our most familiar garden flowers, including snowdrops (*Galanthus*), daffodils (*Narcissus*), lilies (*Lilium*), tulips (*Tulipa*) and many irises, develop from bulbs; crocuses, freesias and gladioli grow from corms. Bulbs are composed of layers of swollen leaf bases, and tend to be moist and juicy, whereas corms are the swollen base of a single stem and tend to be drier. These organs act as a built-in food store. Unfortunately, this also makes them very attractive to pests and diseases in and out of the ground.

BIRD AND ANIMAL PROBLEMS

Dormant bulbs and corms in the garden are a popular target for pheasants and

Bulbs are a rich food store and attract a range of pests.

other **large birds**, while **small mammals**, including mice, voles and squirrels, will take them from the ground or from storage. Larger animals, such as badgers and foxes, may also uproot bulbs through their digging activities. Crocuses seem to be a particular target. Barriers are the only effective means of protecting bulbs in the garden. Small-mesh wire netting pegged on the surface of the soil, or over the top of containers, should offer good protection. It can be removed once the plants start to grow, as they become much less attractive at this stage. Protect stored bulbs in wooden or cardboard boxes with lids, or by hanging in net bags. Do not use plastic boxes or bags, because these trap moisture and encourage rotting.

Sparrows sometimes attack crocus flowers, tearing them to pieces. They can be deterred by pushing twigs between the bulbs and crisscrossing them with black thread. Make sure this is cotton, and easily broken, so the birds cannot be permanently entangled.

TUNNELLING PESTS

If established daffodil bulbs fail to come up, or just produce a few thin or distorted leaves, lift a couple of bulbs and cut them open. An individual grub confirms attack by the **large narcissus fly**. This fly is furry, like a small bumble bee, and can be very destructive. The fly lays its eggs on the neck of bulbs as the foliage dies down, so mounding up soil around the base or covering bulbs with horticultural fleece or insect-proof mesh will thwart it. There is no chemical treatment, and affected bulbs should be dug out and destroyed. Large narcissus fly also attacks snowdrops and hippeastrums, though bulbs grown in the shade are less likely to be attacked. You may also find a number of small maggots. These are larvae of the **small narcissus fly**, but they only attack bulbs that are already damaged.

*A bulb with a hollow centre filled with droppings and a large, fat, off-white grub has been attacked by **large narcissus fly**.*

*Streaked and distorted foliage, and concentric, dark rings or arcs inside the bulb are symptoms of **narcissus eelworm**.*

If, instead of maggots, you find concentric, brown rings when you cut open the bulb, this is likely to be caused by **narcissus eelworm**. These microscopic nematodes invade the

59

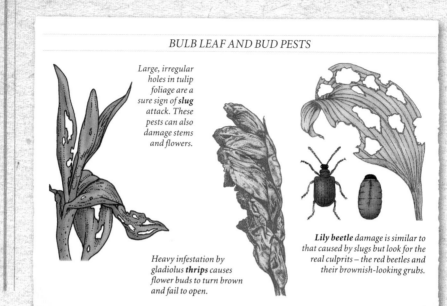

Large, irregular holes in tulip foliage are a sure sign of **slug** *attack. These pests can also damage stems and flowers.*

Heavy infestation by gladiolus **thrips** *causes flower buds to turn brown and fail to open.*

Lily beetle *damage is similar to that caused by slugs but look for the real culprits – the red beetles and their brownish-looking grubs.*

60

whole plant, weakening and eventually killing it. If you diagnose eelworm in a patch of daffodils, all the bulbs within 1m (3ft) are likely to be affected too, and should be removed. Narcissus eelworm also affects snowdrops, hyacinths (*Hyacinthus*) and bluebells (*Hyacinthoides*).

SHOOT-EATING PESTS

Slugs and **snails** are very partial to juicy bulb foliage and will also attack the flowers and the bulbs themselves. Growing bulbs in pots is one solution, especially if you stand the container on pot feet, or use copper tape, to deter interlopers. Otherwise, use slug pellets or powders, parasitic nematodes (in warm, damp weather), hand picking at night or beer traps (see p43).

Lily beetles and their larvae can cause enormous damage to lilies and fritillaries (*Fritillaria*). The adult beetles are about 8mm (⅓ in) long, vivid red with black heads, legs and underparts. The larvae are dull red but camouflage themselves with their greenish black droppings. The adults emerge from the soil in mid- or late spring, and thorough hand picking of adults and their eggs at this stage may control them. Beetles drop to the ground when approached, so spread

*Crown imperial (*Fritillaria imperialis*) can be a target for lily beetle.*

They feed on plant sap and do little damage in small numbers. However, in hot, dry weather, large numbers can build up and can weaken plants; these insects can be especially damaging to flowers. Thrips can swarm on affected plants, and damaged areas show up as silvery streaks or spots. Treat heavy infestations of this sap-sucking pest with a suitable insecticide.

a white cloth under the plants first, so you can still spot them. If larvae appear, then more drastic measures are needed, and they can be treated successfully with appropriate insecticides.

SAP-SUCKING PESTS

Aphids often cluster on the tips of emerging bulbs, especially tulips, and can cause significant damage. They do less direct harm to mature plants, but carry viral diseases that are damaging, so should be controlled where practical. There are several suitable insecticides, or aphids can be squashed by hand (see p40). Use a soft brush to remove aphids attacking stored bulbs.

Thrips are tiny, flying insects, pale or dark brown and barely 2mm (1/12in) long. At rest, they fold their wings back to create a very narrow appearance.

NON-FLOWERING BULBS

Newly planted bulbs that do not flower in their first year may simply be too small and immature to produce flowers. Left another year, with enough food and moisture, they should bloom properly. Older, non-flowering bulbs that otherwise appear healthy may have become overcrowded so that there is too much competition for available resources in the soil. Water with a liquid feed to help build up the bulbs. Once the foliage has died down, lift them and remove all the very small bulbs. Replant the rest at least two to three bulb-widths apart. Bulb fly (see p59) and basal rot (see p63) will also prevent flowering, though leaf development is also likely to be affected.

STORAGE PROBLEMS

You may need to store bulbs and corms between buying them and planting them, or if you use them for temporary displays in containers and beds, in which case they should be lifted for reuse and kept **frost** free over winter. It's important to remember that bulbs and corms are living things, so they should not be subjected to extremes of temperature or very dry conditions, which leads to **shrivelling**. Nor should they be stored in a sealed container, which encourages **rotting**. Netting bags hung up in a cool shed or garage work well for small quantities; for large amounts, use slatted trays, but make sure mice can't get to them.

Dry bulbs off carefully before storage and check stored bulbs regularly, so you can remove any that become soft, show signs of mould or become hard, dry and chalky. If you still have problems with rotting, dust the bulbs and corms with sulphur before storage. **Blue mould** is a typical storage rot, caused by the same type of fungus (penicillium) that causes blue mould on cheese. Always discard affected bulbs, and improve ventilation.

BULB ROTS IN THE GARDEN

Bulbs that come from cool climates, such as daffodils, bluebells and snowdrops, are reasonably tolerant of moist conditions. However, those from hotter, drier areas, such as tulips, may well rot in heavy, cold, damp soils.

Tulip grey bulb rot, which also affects hyacinths, daffodils, gladioli and several other bulbs, lives in the soil and attacks bulbs as they start to grow. Sometimes, the bulb is killed even before the shoot emerges above ground level. If the bulbs are left in the soil, the fungus will remain to contaminate other bulbs, so when bulbs fail to grow it's always worth checking what has happened. If tulip grey bulb rot is the problem, remove any bulb debris, and the soil immediately around it, and consign it to the dustbin. Avoid planting bulbs in the area for several years.

BULB STORAGE PROBLEMS

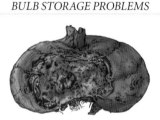

Blue mould, *shown here on gladiolus, can affect most bulbs. It starts as a brown, sunken area, which first produces pink or buff spores then a blue, mouldy coating.*

62

BULB ROTS IN THE GARDEN

Tulip grey bulb rot *starts as a dry, grey rot then spreads as a whitish mould that carries large, black spore bodies up to 7mm (¼in) across.*

Symptoms of narcissus **basal rot** *are a softened base and red, rotten areas inside the bulb.*

Daffodils can be attacked by **basal rot** in late spring, when the roots are naturally dying back. If left in the soil, the bulb will disintegrate and the fungus will spread to neighbouring bulbs. Lifting and destroying affected bulbs is the only treatment. When lifted, bulbs may look sound at first, but they may then go soft and they should therefore be discarded.

Onion white rot can be very damaging not only to onions (see p130) but

also to ornamental varieties of alliums – the onion family. It attacks the plants while in growth, rotting the roots and the base of the bulb and covering the affected tissues with white, fluffy growth. Affected plants cannot be saved and should be destroyed. Do not

Daffodils naturalise well, but don't let them get overcrowded.

Plant tulips in late autumn, to reduce the risk of tulip fire.

grow alliums in the same site in future, because onion white rot lingers in the soil for many years.

LEAF AND FLOWER DISEASES

Small **leaf spots** (see p46) may just indicate minor fungal infections, and picking off the worst affected leaves is all the action you need to take in this case. However, if the unsightly spots become larger and affect substantial parts of the leaf, then the problem may be more serious, and you should treat the disease as appropriate. Significant bulb diseases that produce leaf spots as a symptom include lily disease, gladiolus scab and tulip fire.

In damp conditions, **lily disease** can develop rapidly, killing leaves and spreading to stems and flowers. Cut off and destroy affected growth to control this disease. Good growing conditions help avoid the problem, so make sure to grow lilies in well-drained soil with good air circulation.

Gladiolus scab starts as small, red-brown spots, but these enlarge and darken. Leaf tips go brown, and shoots may rot at ground level. If lifted, the gladiolus corms have circular depressions on the base, oozing with yellow gum that later becomes dry and shiny. Burn diseased plants, and do not use the area again for gladioli, or for freesias and crocus which are also susceptible to this bacterial disease.

Tulip fire is a common and serious disease of tulips. It starts with brown scorching at the tips of young leaves, which may then rot and die. If the leaves do survive, they develop small, pale brown spots, which also appear on the flowers and affect neighbouring plants, too. Dig up and destroy affected bulbs and avoid planting tulips in the area for three years. Planting tulips in late autumn, rather than earlier in the growing season, makes attacks by the fungus that causes tulip fire less likely.

Brown tips on daffodil leaves may just be caused by **cold** or **dryness,** but if they appear burnt or scorched this suggests fungal **leaf scorch**. Remove and destroy the tips. Once dormant, lift the bulbs and dust with sulphur to help control the problem in future. Leaf scorch also affects hippeastrum, crinum, nerine and snowdrops.

Snowdrops sometimes develop a covering of **grey mould**, which is caused by a fungus that attacks only snowdrops. This disease, which is worse in mild winters, seriously stunts growth and ultimately rots the bulb. Lift and destroy affected clumps.

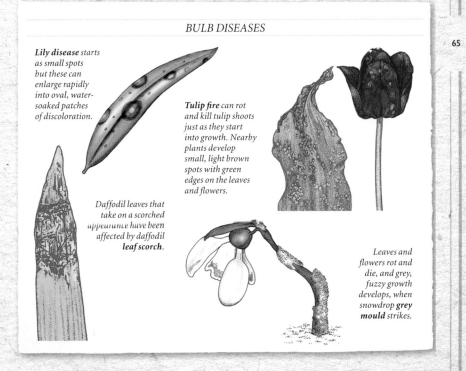

BULB DISEASES

Lily disease starts as small spots but these can enlarge rapidly into oval, water-soaked patches of discoloration.

Tulip fire can rot and kill tulip shoots just as they start into growth. Nearby plants develop small, light brown spots with green edges on the leaves and flowers.

Daffodil leaves that take on a scorched appearance have been affected by daffodil leaf scorch.

Leaves and flowers rot and die, and grey, fuzzy growth develops, when snowdrop grey mould strikes.

• GLASSHOUSE PLANTS •

Healthy plants are more able to resist the pests and diseases that also thrive in this sheltered situation, where conditions should be kept as consistent as possible.

ENVIRONMENTAL PROBLEMS

Plants are easily **scorched** when grown under glass, so protect them during the hottest months with glasshouse shading paint, netting or blinds.

Erratic water supplies can lead to **flower buds aborting** and to **blossom end rot** in tomatoes and peppers (see p140). Moving plants into larger containers may help, as may setting up an automatic watering system.

High humidity coupled with little air movement encourage diseases,

Good hygiene helps prevent many glasshouse problems.

so ventilation is important. The lush growing environment of the glasshouse can also highlight problems with **mineral deficiency**, so always use a good-quality compost supplemented by slow-release or liquid fertiliser.

PEST PROBLEMS

Glasshouse whiteflies and their larvae feed by sucking sap and can weaken plants. They excrete large quantities of surplus sugar as a sticky liquid called honeydew, which is disfiguring when colonised by black **sooty mould** (see p90). Although sooty mould does not

Carnation tortrix larvae are small, yellow or green, and hide away by joining leaves together with strands of silk.

Glasshouse whiteflies are tiny flies with white wings. When disturbed, they rise up in a cloud. Their immobile larvae are white, flattened and scale-like.

Despite their name, *glasshouse red spider mites* are usually yellow-green with two black spots. They turn red only when hibernating.

Mealybugs look like miniature woodlice, up to 7mm ($\frac{5}{16}$in) long. They cover themselves in fluffy, white wax scales so are easy to mistake for fungal growth.

67

Glasshouse *leafhoppers* live on the undersides of leaves, jumping off when disturbed. Affected leaves develop coarse, pale mottling, which can eventually cover the whole leaf.

Sciarid flies are small and slow-moving, often crawling on the compost surface. The soil-dwelling maggots are white with a black head and up to 3mm ($\frac{1}{8}$in) long.

harm the plants directly, it can build up so thickly on leaves that their ability to photosynthesise is reduced. Yellow sticky traps put in place at the start of the season may catch enough whitefly to stop numbers building up. If they do become a problem, then biological control using the tiny parasitic wasp *Encarsia* can be very effective (see p44). Alternatively, control whitefly by spraying with a suitable insecticide.

Glasshouse red spider mites are only just visible to the naked eye, and move around very slowly. The first symptom is a light mottling or speckling of the leaves, which can then turn brown and die. Small wisps of webbing may also be visible. Badly infested plants can be killed. Spider mites thrive in a hot, dry atmosphere, so reducing the heat and increasing humidity deters them. Pesticide sprays can be effective. Otherwise, introduce the fast-moving, predatory mite *Phytoseiulus* as biological control (see p42).

Aphids, especially the peach-potato aphid which may be green, pink or yellow-green, thrive in glasshouses, distorting shoot tips, weakening plant growth and covering foliage with sticky honeydew that attracts sooty mould. For control see p40.

Mealybugs (see p67) tend to attack slower-growing plants, and often hide in inaccessible places. Isolate affected plants and treat with a suitable insecticide.

Leafhoppers (see p67) are a particular problem on primulas, but attack many plants including tomatoes, fuchsias and pelargoniums. Control them with suitable insecticides.

Slugs and **snails** (see p43) enjoy glasshouse life safe from predators and can be very damaging to young plants.

A few caterpillars spend their lives in glasshouses, though the damage is rarely serious. The large, yellow-green to brown **tomato moth** caterpillar attacks the leaves and fruit of tomatoes, sweet peppers and cucumbers (see p140), while the **carnation tortrix moth** caterpillar (see p67) affects many glasshouse plants as well as shrubs out of doors. Hand picking is usually sufficient to control these two pests.

Sciarid flies (see p67), also known as fungus gnats, are attracted to moist compost to lay their eggs. The larvae feed mainly on dead material, but may attack the roots of seedlings or the base of cuttings. Allowing the compost surface to dry out between waterings helps deter them. Yellow sticky traps will catch the adults, and soil insecticide will control the larvae where necessary.

Vine weevil grubs (see p44) attack plant roots, and the bases of shoots, and their activities often go unnoticed until the affected plant suddenly collapses. The larvae thrive in composts based on organic material such as peat or bark, so are a particular problem in containers.

DISEASE PROBLEMS

Grey mould usually begins by attacking dead or dying foliage or flowers but can easily spread to healthy material such as cuttings or young plants. **Downy mildew** (see p45) is also a killer, especially of seedlings, starting as discoloration of the tissues that can rapidly disintegrate into slime.

Rusts can be controlled if caught in good time. Chrysanthemums can develop both **white rust** and **brown rust**. Destroy affected plants and spray neighbouring ones with a suitable fungicide. **Fuchsia rust** produces small spots, yellow on the upper leaf surface, dark brown underneath. **Pelargonium rust** also produces yellow marks on the upper surface of the leaf and brown rings with a central spot underneath. These types of rust are less serious and can often be controlled by removing affected leaves, though fungicide treatment may also be needed.

Powdery mildew (see p47) appears as grey or white patches, which can spread to cover the whole leaf surface. Spraying with an appropriate fungicide may help control the disease.

Viruses can occur in many plants grown in glasshouses including orchids, vegetable crops, bedding plants and pot plants. **Cucumber mosaic virus** (see p124) attacks many plants including begonia, cyclamen, hoya, petunia and primulas. It produces yellow mottling on the leaves often accompanied by distortion to leaves, flowers and fruit. **Tobacco mosaic virus**, which can be transmitted by handling cigarettes, also affects brugmansia, aubergine,

*Areas affected by **grey mould** darken, develop a furry, grey coating, then rot.*

__Chrysanthemum white rust__ produces yellow spots on the upper surface and pale brown pustules on the underside of the leaf.

69

capsicums and petunias and causes leaf mottling and distortion together with breaks in flower colour. Virus in orchids is usually characterised by black streaks or spots. Some plants survive successfully with viral infection: for example, it is responsible for the attractive mottling in variegated abutilons. Viruses cannot be treated, so destroy adversely affected plants.

The term 'herbaceous perennial' can be applied to any plant that lives for several years, but dies down to the ground for a period every year. This is normally winter in cooler climates, but may be summer in hot, dry climates. This annual loss of top growth is a good way for plants to divest themselves of old, damaged or diseased foliage. The drawback is that the spring growth is particularly vulnerable to pests and inclement weather, while foliage that is past its peak often succumbs to disease.

ROOT PESTS

Swift moth caterpillars are unusual in feeding entirely below ground, on plant roots. They do a certain amount

Planting a mix of perennials helps minimise the impact of any problems.

of damage, but often go unnoticed until plants are lifted prior to division, when the larvae can be removed and destroyed. The moths are deterred from egg-laying by patches of bare earth, so keeping the ground free of weeds helps reduce the problem.

Cutworms (see p55) may also feed on herbaceous perennials at or near the soil surface, but they are unlikely to do significant damage to established plants.

If plants with fleshy crowns suddenly collapse, as though short of water, try pulling on the foliage. If it comes away from the ground, the problem is likely to be **vine weevil** larvae eating the crown and roots and severing the shoots. The small, cream grubs, curled up in a C-shape, will be seen in the damaged areas of the plants and in the surrounding soil. Among herbaceous plants, vine weevils particularly attack heuchera, saxifrage and sedum. The adults feed on leaves (see p73). Remove and destroy any grubs you find. There are no pesticides available for garden use, only for plants growing in containers. Treat bad vine weevil infestations by biological control using nematodes (see p44). These carry bacteria that are fatal to the grubs.

ROOT DISEASES

Root rots are caused by soilborne fungi that turn plant roots and crowns black and rotten. The leaves of affected plants become discoloured from the top of the shoot downwards, and if damage underground is serious all the top growth dies back as a result. Confirm the cause by lifting plants with these symptoms and checking the roots. Chrysanthemums, delphiniums, gentians, lupins, Michaelmas daisies (*Aster novi-belgii*) and primulas are prone to this problem. Destroy badly affected plants.

ROOT PROBLEMS

Swift moth *larvae live among plant roots. They have off-white bodies and red-brown heads and can grow up to 4cm (1½in) long.*

Although chrysanthemum **root rot** *blackens and destroys roots and crowns, it is often first noticed when shoots start to die back from the top down.*

71

LEAF AND SHOOT PESTS

Capsid bugs (see p72) are like giant greenfly, 5mm (¼in) or more in length, and are highly mobile, with long legs. They extract sap from buds and young shoots, producing toxins that kill small areas of leaf tissue. As the leaf expands, these areas tear into jagged, irregular holes. By the time this damage is spotted, the capsids are usually long gone. If damage occurs regularly, spray susceptible plants in spring with a suitable

Phlox eelworms *themselves cannot be seen, but their presence results in characteristic distortion to leaves and stems.*

Cuckoo spit *appears as a white, foamy blob, protecting one or more pale green or pale orange froghopper nymphs.*

Capsid bug *damage, seen here on a dahlia, appears as ragged holes and distorted growth.*

72

insecticide. Chrysanthemums and dahlias are particular targets for capsid bugs.

Adult froghoppers are hard-coated insects that leap away when disturbed, but the young nymphs are soft and vulnerable, so protect themselves with a white froth known as **cuckoo spit**. In clusters, froghoppers can distort stem tips and damage growth. Hand pick or spray with a suitable insecticide.

Eelworms are microscopic nematodes that live inside plants but can move around from plant to plant in wet conditions. Phlox is prone to this problem, which also affects gypsophila, evening primrose (*Oenothera*) and sweet Williams (*Dianthus barbatus*). Destroy

affected plants and do not replant in the same area for two years.

Slugs and **snails** are attracted to young shoots and can be a particular problem with delphiniums, dianthus, hostas, lupins and red lobelia, where they can destroy almost all the new growth, or leave foliage full of ragged holes.

Different species of sawfly larvae tend to be quite specific about what plants they attack, and a few feed exclusively on small groups of herbaceous plants. **Solomon's seal sawfly**, which may also attack lily of the valley (*Convallaria*), strips the leaves back to their midribs, seemingly overnight. Hand picking can help. Otherwise, spray with a suitable insecticide. Geum, aquilegia and goatsbeard (*Aruncus dioicus*) have their own sawfly pests.

Damage by **earwigs** is unlikely to affect a plant's overall health. Earwigs are fast-moving and feed at night. Trap them by placing a flowerpot filled with dry grass on a cane among affected plants. The earwigs will shelter in the trap during the daytime, and can be shaken out in another area of the garden.

Deep notches cut in the edge of leaves indicates the activities of adult **vine weevils** (see p44). They have a particular fondness for bergenias. The damage to leaves is essentially cosmetic – it's the larvae that do real damage by feeding on roots (see p71). Adults are wingless, but walk long distances at night, so find and destroy them by torchlight.

Large numbers of small, ragged holes in young growth of figwort (*Scrophularia*), phygelius or verbascum are the work of **figwort weevils** and their larvae. The adults are about 4mm (⅛in) long, black with pale mottling, and the

---

LEAF-EATING PESTS

*Large, ragged holes are often the work of **slugs** or **snails**. Slime trails confirm this but are not always easy to spot.*

*Solomon's seal **sawfly** larvae are blue-grey, up to 2cm (¾in) long and generally found in clusters.*

__Earwigs__ feed at night so are rarely spotted while they nibble small holes in leaves and flowers.

grubs are brownish yellow. Pick off badly affected shoots and, if necessary, spray with a suitable insecticide.

SPOTS, LINES AND BLOTCHES CAUSED BY PESTS

Most mature herbaceous plants develop a certain amount of **discoloration** on the leaves, which may be due to pest attack, physical damage by weather, nutrient problems or disease. A great many of these problems can be ignored, especially towards the end of the season, or treated simply by improving the plants' growing conditions.

Pale wavy lines or translucent blotches show the activities of leaf-mining grubs. These are the larvae of a variety of insects: **chrysanthemum leaf miners** and **delphinium leaf miners** grow up to be flies, and **geum leaf miners** are immature sawflies. Holding a leaf up to the light often reveals the larvae. Destroying affected leaves can help reduce pest numbers. There is no suitable insecticide.

Large, dark spots sharply defined between leaf veins are likely to be caused by **eelworms**. These microscopic nematodes kill off patches of tissue but cannot cross the larger veins. They tend to affect the lower leaves first, but can spread upwards rapidly in wet weather. There is no chemical treatment, and badly affected plants should be dug up and destroyed. Susceptible plants include chrysanthemum, Japanese anemone (*Anemone × hybrida*), paeony (*Paeonia*) and penstemon.

SPOTS, LINES AND BLOTCHES CAUSED BY DISEASES

Leaf spots and **blotches** should be taken more seriously if they appear before the middle of the growing season, if they occur mainly on young leaves or if they spread rapidly to the point where growth or health are adversely affected.

Iris leaf spot can kill leaves if allowed to get established and this in turn weakens plants and reduces flowering. Remove affected foliage promptly. Weak growth and wet conditions favour the disease; sturdy plants growing in a sunny area are less susceptible.

Powdery mildew is very common, and is particularly likely to attack plants that are stressed by lack of water. If it appears early in the season, spray with a suitable fungicide and improve soil moisture levels by watering and mulching. If powdery mildew appears late in the year, burn or bin affected foliage. With very vulnerable plants such as Michaelmas daisies it's well worth choosing resistant varieties.

Delphinium black blotch is caused by bacteria. It starts on the leaves but can spread to stems and flowers. No chemical control is available. Remove affected leaves promptly.

Hellebores can suffer from **leaf spots**, which start small then join up into blotches. Control their spread by removing affected leaves.

A much more serious condition is **hellebore black death**. Destroy any plant affected by this virus.

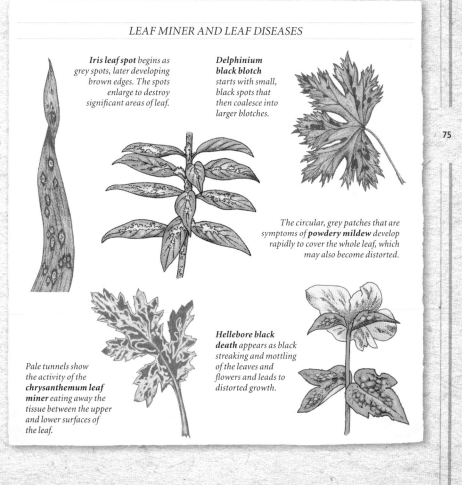

LEAF MINER AND LEAF DISEASES

Iris leaf spot begins as grey spots, later developing brown edges. The spots enlarge to destroy significant areas of leaf.

Delphinium black blotch starts with small, black spots that then coalesce into larger blotches.

*The circular, grey patches that are symptoms of **powdery mildew** develop rapidly to cover the whole leaf, which may also become distorted.*

*Pale tunnels show the activity of the **chrysanthemum leaf miner** eating away the tissue between the upper and lower surfaces of the leaf.*

Hellebore black death appears as black streaking and mottling of the leaves and flowers and leads to distorted growth.

FLOWER PESTS

Leaf-eating pests, including **slugs** and **caterpillars**, are often equally happy eating flowers so are likely culprits if flowers disappear or have large holes in them. Much smaller pests can also result in significant damage.

Varieties of day lily (*Hemerocallis*) that flower in early summer can suffer from **hemerocallis gall midge**. These tiny flies lay their eggs in the buds. Feeding by the resultant maggots distorts and kills the buds. The maggots can be seen if the buds are cut open. Remove and destroy affected buds.

Tiny **gall mites** can infest the tips of Michaelmas daisies, and the plant responds by producing a mass of small

Early-flowering day lilies (Hemerocallis) can be attacked by hemerocallis gall midges.

leaves rather than flowers. Plants may show other damage, such as scarring on the stems,. Remove and destroy badly affected plants. *Aster novae-angliae* and *A. amellus* are more resistant to this mite than *A. novi-belgii*.

FLOWER DISEASES

Chrysanthemums are susceptible to several viruses, but **aspermy virus** is the most serious. It is spread by aphids, and its main symptom is small, distorted flowers with uneven petals. Destroy affected plants and control aphids to prevent transmission to new plants.

Peony wilt is a form of rot that can affect stems and leaves but is most noticeable when it attacks flower buds. These turn brown and fail to open, and can become covered in furry, grey

---

DIVIDING PERENNIALS

Most herbaceous perennials form gradually spreading clumps, which tend to use up available soil nutrients and soil moisture. Overall vigour declines, flowers and foliage get smaller and clumps often start to die off in the centre. To reverse this trend, dig up plants in autumn after they have died down, or in spring before they have made much growth. Pull them apart or cut into smaller pieces, retaining the young vigorous parts. Before replanting, dig in bulky organic material.

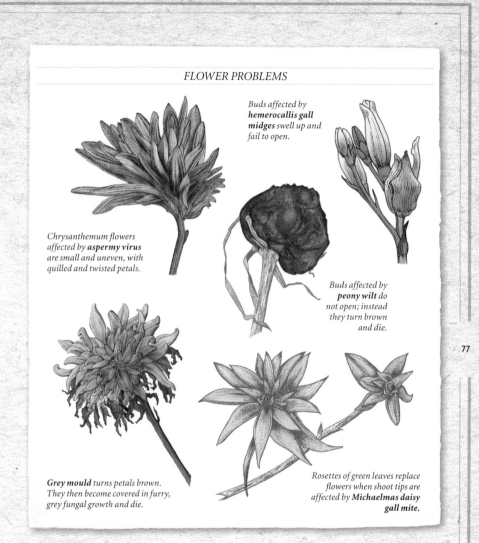

Buds affected by **hemerocallis gall midges** swell up and fail to open.

*Chrysanthemum flowers affected by **aspermy virus** are small and uneven, with quilled and twisted petals.*

Buds affected by **peony wilt** do not open; instead they turn brown and die.

Grey mould turns petals brown. They then become covered in furry, grey fungal growth and die.

Rosettes of green leaves replace flowers when shoot tips are affected by **Michaelmas daisy gall mite.**

77

mould. Cut out affected shoots, below soil level, and dispose of them. Thinning out shoots to improve air circulation can help keep the disease at bay.

Flowers growing in very humid conditions, or wet from rain, can succumb to **grey mould**. Petals turn brown, then rot, and may develop fuzzy, grey fungal growths. This disease will be localised within the affected tissues so if dead material is cut out the rest of the plant should be unaffected.

Renovating a poor-looking lawn can transform the appearance of your garden.

Regular maintenance is the key to a healthy, attractive lawn.

GENERAL APPEARANCE

Cut back **overgrown** grass initially to 5cm (2in) and clear away all the cuttings. Cut the lawn again, gradually reducing the height to about 2cm (¾in) for a family lawn and 1cm (½in) for a fine lawn. Fine lawns will need cutting twice a week when growing strongly, family lawns once a week. Leave the grass longer in very dry periods and over winter.

Poor overall colour often indicates a hungry lawn. Treat with a liquid feed, which acts quickly, or more economically use a granular feed distributed by hand or applicator.

Fill small **hollows** by adding a layer of sieved soil and sand up to 1cm (½in) deep. When the grass has grown through, another layer can be added. **Bumps** and larger hollows should be treated by cutting a cross into the turf centred over the problem area. Carefully undercut the turf and peel it back. Then add or remove soil as necessary before replacing the turf. Fill in any gaps and water well.

Some gardeners are more than happy to see **weeds**, or wild flowers, in the lawn but for others they destroy that perfect finish. Cut out individual weeds with an old knife, or treat them with a spot weedkiller. If all-over treatment is needed, mark out the area first with string or canes so that you can apply the product accurately. Use a watering-can with a dribble bar, and keep it just for this purpose. Ideally, weedkiller should be applied a week or so after fertiliser application, but there are many combined weed and feed products, which can save time. Sometimes, lawns are invaded by weed grasses such as coarse cocksfoot (*Dactylis glomerata*), pale Yorkshire fog (*Holcus lanatus*) or annual meadow grass (*Poa annua*),

which dies off in winter. Lawn weedkiller will not kill them, nor the related sedges and rushes, so remove these by hand. (See pp183–185 for some more typical lawn weeds.)

Some **moss** is inevitable in all but the finest, most cosseted lawns, but if it begins to take over then action needs to be taken. Vigorous raking with a lawn rake can remove large quantities of moss, but it will generally return, so treatment with mosskiller may be needed. Water this on, then rake out the dead moss a week or so later. Lush growth of moss usually indicates areas

IMPROVING A POOR LAWN

Regular mowing, to an appropriate height, is the most important factor in maintaining a healthy lawn.

Spring feeding encourages thick, healthy turf that is better able to resist diseases and crowd out weeds.

Scarifying (raking hard) in autumn will not only collect up fallen tree leaves but also remove dead grass and moss, opening up the turf to let in air and moisture.

Topdress in autumn with sandy loam to help produce the level surface needed for even turf.

that are shady and damp. If these conditions can be improved – for example, by cutting back overhanging plants or improving drainage – then moss should be less of a problem.

Where grass growth is very weak, through soil compaction or lack of feeding, **lichen** (see p81) may develop. This scaly plant is brown and soft when moist, black and crisp when dry. It is easily scraped off the surface. Improving the growing conditions for the grass should prevent lichen returning.

PEST-PROBLEMS

Dead patches in an otherwise healthy lawn are often due to insect pests. **Chafer grubs** do most damage, severing grass roots so the top growth just pulls away. **Foxes**, **badgers** and **crows** can then root around after the grubs and cause more damage. Chafer grubs can live for several years underground, depending on the conditions, but eventually develop into **chafer beetles**.

Leatherjackets also feed on grass roots and attract birds such as starlings to feed on them. They develop into crane flies (daddy-long-legs). Both these pests can be controlled by applying a suitable soil insecticide or by using biological control by nematodes, though each pest requires a different species.

Earthworms are generally beneficial in gardens, and their tunnelling and recycling activities are also helpful to lawns, so they should be tolerated. Some earthworms produce piles of soil on the surface, and these casts can be dispersed with a brush when dry.

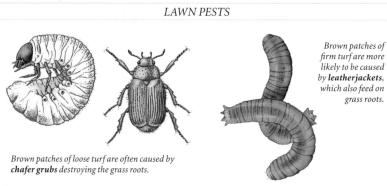

LAWN PESTS

*Brown patches of firm turf are more likely to be caused by **leatherjackets**, which also feed on grass roots.*

*Brown patches of loose turf are often caused by **chafer grubs** destroying the grass roots.*

Some species of **ants** build their nests in lawns and can create bumps on the surface. Sweep away the soil whenever you see it, and lower bumps if necessary (see p78). Ant colonies can be destroyed with pesticides or boiling water, but they are likely to return so are best tolerated.

Moles can create a lot of damage in lawns by tunnelling below the surface and throwing up heaps of soil into molehills. Trapping can be an effective option, but neighbouring moles are likely to move into the vacated territory.

DISEASE PROBLEMS

Fusarium patch tends to appear during mild weather in spring and autumn. It can be encouraged by over-application of fertiliser, creating soft growth, or by still, damp conditions under overhanging foliage. Spraying with an appropriate fungicide may help. The disease is usually not seen in drier weather.

A wide range of toadstools can appear in lawns. These are the fruiting bodies of fungi that live underground, usually quite harmlessly, feeding on dead organic material in the soil. They can be swept away or left to die down naturally. However, **fairy ring fungi** can cause problems as they create distinct, dark rings, or arcs, in the lawn. Sometimes

LAWN DISEASES AND LICHEN

Patches of yellow, dying grass with pink or white, mouldy growth indicate **fusarium patch**, also called snow mould.

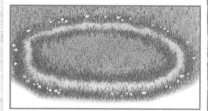

Dark rings or partial rings in the lawn are symptoms of the **fairy ring fungus**.

Compact soil and poor drainage encourage the growth of **lichen**. Scrape it off, then improve cultural conditions to discourage regrowth.

parts of the ring turn brown as the fungus repels water and deprives the grass of moisture. The only treatment available is to dig out the ring to a depth of at least 30cm (12in), and to 30cm (12in) beyond the ring. Fill with fresh soil and sow grass seed or returf.

Trees-and shrubs are in it for the long haul. Most shrubs live at least ten years, and trees may live for several hundred. This means they have considerable reserves, especially in their permanent roots and branches, and can shake off many pest and disease problems that would seriously threaten more short-lived plants. However, their longevity does mean they suffer from pests such as scale insects and diseases such as honey fungus that tend to build up over time and rarely threaten annual or herbaceous plants. Their large size also means that if they become unhealthy they could become unsafe so always investigate symptoms of serious diseases and, where necessary, seek professional

Most trees and shrubs are resilient and will shrug off many problems.

advice. Trees and shrubs vary greatly in their tolerance of different growing conditions with some seeming to thrive anywhere and others having very specific requirements, especially in terms of soil pH. Whatever a plant needs, it will grow better in an appropriate environment and so will suffer fewer problems from pests or diseases.

ENVIRONMENTAL PROBLEMS
Distorted leaves and shoots appearing early in the year, with no obvious pest or disease symptoms, may well be due to weather damage, especially **frost**

and cold wind. This kills off some of the tissues, leaving scars that distort subsequent growth. In summer, browning of young growth, or leaves on vulnerable shade-lovers such as Japanese maples (*Acer japonicum*, *A. palmatum*), together with brown spots on yellow-leaved plants can all be due to **scorch** by sunlight or warm, drying winds. Sometimes these problems cannot be prevented, but careful siting of plants in the first place can help avoid them, and fleece covers provide temporary shelter during inclement periods.

Sometimes, frost damage produces a curious effect known as **fasciation**, where stems become flattened, and sometimes twisted. Damage by insects or mechanical injury can have the same effect. Normally only one or two shoots

LIME-INDUCED CHLOROSIS

Some shrubs develop yellowy leaves if the soil is too alkaline.

Most shrubs are reasonably tolerant of soil pH, that is the degree of acidity or alkalinity in the soil, which is determined by its lime content. The neutral point is pH7. In gardens, acid soils may be pH4–6.5 and alkaline soils pH7.5–8.5. Some shrubs will thrive only when planted in soils with a low pH; in neutral or alkaline soils, they are unable to absorb enough iron from the soil and so develop a yellowing of the leaves, known as lime-induced chlorosis, and do not grow vigorously. In severe cases, leaves may turn brown and the plants become stunted and die. Among the most sensitive plants are heathers and rhododendrons, which need pH5 or less, whereas skimmias and camellias can tolerate pH6. If chlorosis is only mild, you can boost the iron available to plants by watering on compounds containing chelated iron, which is not locked up by the lime in the soil. Otherwise, grow lime-haters in containers of low pH (ericaceous) compost. Adding hard tap water may still lead to chlorosis, so use rainwater as much as possible.

DISTORTED GROWTH

Mis-shapen or curved leaves, such as on this camellia, can develop in response to **frost** damage.

Fasciation on forsythia appears like a bundle of shoots fused together, but still producing leaves and flowers.

are affected and can be pruned out. A few plants such as *Salix sachalinensis* 'Sekka' are specifically grown for this effect and in this case the distortion is genetic.

PROBLEMS WITH DIE-BACK

When trees or shrubs start to die back wholesale, then problems at the roots are the most likely cause. Check for excessive wet or dryness, or physical damage, first. The next most likely cause is a root rot/wilt disease: **honey fungus** (see p46), **phytophthora** (see p47) or **verticillium wilt** (see p49). With cotoneaster, hawthorn (*Crataegus*) and related species suspect **fireblight** (see p153).

BRANCH AND TRUNK PESTS

Many types of scale insect attack trees and shrubs. Some are limited to a small number of species, such as **beech scale**, which forms conspicuous areas of white, wax powder on trunks and branches and only attacks beech trees, and **euonymus scale**, which attacks only euonymus and can build up into such thick clusters that it looks like part of the bark. On the other hand, **horse chestnut scale** and **willow scale** (see p86) attack a wide range of trees and shrubs.

Brown scale (see p161), also known as peach scale, is a significant pest of peaches,

Maples need more care than some trees, but the display is worth it.

SCALE INSECTS

Horse chestnut scales are 4mm (⅛in) or more across, and dark brown, and each one rests on a white egg mass.

Although relatively small, at 2–3mm (¹⁄₁₂–⅛in) across, willow scales can cluster so closely together that stems appear whitewashed.

but has been recorded on more than 300 different ornamental plants. Colonies develop on shoots and leaves as well as woody stems, and the brown, domed scales can be up to 5mm (¼in) long.

BRANCH AND TRUNK DISEASE PROBLEMS

Coral spot fungus can attack a wide range of plants but particularly affects cercis, elaeagnus, magnolia and maple. Although it usually attacks dead wood first, it can spread rapidly to living tissue and can kill badly affected plants. Remove all affected shoots by cutting back into live tissue, and treating immediately with wound paint. Reduce future attacks by pruning carefully, to avoid leaving snags and by removing any dead wood promptly.

Brackets on trunks and large branches are the fruiting bodies of fungi that may have been infecting the tree for many years, so may indicate considerable areas of decay. This can make the tree unstable and unsafe. On the other hand, trees are often able to compartmentalise areas affected by these **wood-rotting fungi** and the damage may be quite localised. It's advisable to seek professional advice when bracket fungi are spotted because of the potential risks of damaged trees falling, or dropping branches.

Trees and shrubs in the *Prunus* family, including flowering almonds and cherries, are susceptible to **bacterial canker.** This causes small, oval craters or cankers on shoots and branches that produce clear, sticky gum. Initially, the branch may still produce leaves, even flowers, but these are likely to be small and sickly, and the branch soon dies back. Bacteria also invade the leaves, producing round, brown spots; the dead tissue then falls away, leaving lots of small holes. Sometimes, trees recover spontaneously, but normally the disease is fatal if left unchecked. If caught early, and all infected shoots cut back into healthy wood, the tree may be saved.

The bacterium responsible for **Horse chestnut bleeding canker** infects the whole tree and can result in die-back, thinning of the crown, yellowing leaves and premature leaf drop as well as oozing from the trunk. There is no treatment, but it does not affect other tree species. Trees may recover, but seek professional advice if they are likely to prove a hazard.

LEAF-EATING PESTS

Quite a range of insects produce holes in the leaves of trees and shrubs but the most significant are caterpillars, sawfly larvae, leaf beetles and their larvae, and capsid bugs.

Both **caterpillars** and **sawfly** larvae can infest trees in huge numbers, but

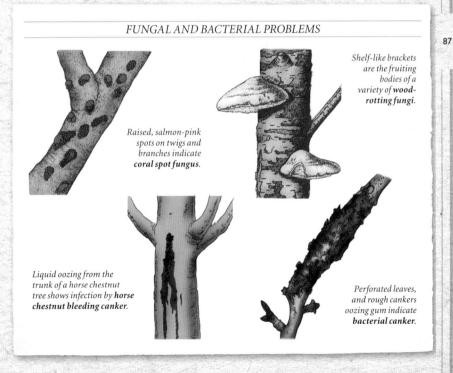

FUNGAL AND BACTERIAL PROBLEMS

*Raised, salmon-pink spots on twigs and branches indicate **coral spot fungus**.*

*Shelf-like brackets are the fruiting bodies of a variety of **wood-rotting fungi**.*

*Liquid oozing from the trunk of a horse chestnut tree shows infection by **horse chestnut bleeding canker**.*

*Perforated leaves, and rough cankers oozing gum indicate **bacterial canker**.*

Buff-tip moth caterpillars feed in groups on various trees and shrubs including hazel, hornbeam, oak, rose and willow.

*Viburnum leaves can be reduced to lace by the activities of **viburnum beetle** and its larvae.*

Horse chestnut leaf miner creates large, disfiguring, brown blotches.

Berberis sawfly can defoliate shrubs very quickly if not controlled.

seem to do little damage to the tree's overall health, while providing an important food supply for many birds. Some caterpillars such as the **buff-tip**, feed on a wide range of plants, but others confine themselves to a few species, and sawflies are usually quite specific too. For example, the **hazel sawfly** is usually found on hazel (*Corylus*) or birch (*Betula*), though it can also feed on maple, hornbeam (*Carpinus*), ash (*Fraxinus*), poplar (*Populus*), willow (*Salix*) and a few other trees. **Berberis sawfly** attacks only berberis and closely related mahonia. If they threaten to defoliate a young tree or shrub or, say, a prized specimen in a container, then these pests are easily controlled by hand picking or by spraying with an appropriate insecticide. Caterpillars can also be controlled by a parasitic nematode (see p41), though this is not effective on sawfly larvae.

Leaf-eating beetles are less ubiquitous, and usually faithful to one type of plant. A common one that feeds on woody plants in gardens is **viburnum beetle**, which first attacks as larvae in spring, then as adults in late summer when these larvae mature. If the newly hatched larvae can be dealt with the damage is relatively minor, but often the problem is not spotted until most of the damage has been done. Suitable systemic insecticides are the most effective treatment, though contact insecticides can help control the larvae.

Leaf miner larvae tunnel between the upper and lower surfaces of a leaf, creating areas of discoloration that are characteristic of individual species. **Lilac**, **holly** and **laburnum leaf miners** produce large, pale blisters in various shapes, and the grubs can sometimes be seen inside. **Horse chestnut leaf miner** produces large, brown blotches that are particularly disfiguring. On small plants, control infestations by picking off and destroying affected leaves; there are no approved insecticides to deal with them. Normally the damage is only cosmetic, though repeated, severe attacks probably do weaken horse chestnuts (*Aesculus*).

Adult **vine weevils** feed on shrubs, especially tough-leaved ones such as camellia, euonymus, rhododendron and skimmia. They cut distinctive, deep, irregular notches around the edges of leaves, normally on the lower branches. This damage is only cosmetic, but if adult weevils are seen they should be disposed of because of the immense damage done to roots by their larvae (see p44).

SAP-SUCKING PESTS

Many type of **aphids** (see p40) feed by sucking sap from shrubs and trees, especially young shoots and the undersides of leaves. On most trees, they seem to have little effect on the tree itself, but the sticky honeydew they produce can be a significant nuisance if it falls on plants, paving or vehicles underneath. Although aphids are susceptible to many pesticides, they cannot be controlled on trees as there is no practical way to apply the appropriate treatment. In the long term, it is best to avoid planting susceptible trees such as lime (*Tilia*), oak (*Quercus*), silver birch (*Betula pendula*), sycamore (*Acer pseudoplatanus*) and willow anywhere that honeydew will cause problems. On some plants, such as flowering cherry (*Prunus*) and

89

viburnum, aphids clustering at shoot tips can cause significant distortion to new growth, and should be controlled by squashing or spraying with appropriate pesticides. It's important to keep a look-out for developing colonies in spring, as control is much more effective in the early stages of infestation.

Capsid bugs feed by sucking sap. They mostly do this while the leaves are still in bud and, at the same time, they inject toxins into the leaf. This creates dead patches, which tear into holes when the leaf expands. Normally, when the damage is seen the capsids have moved on, but, if they regularly cause damage,

treat the affected plants with a suitable systemic insecticide. Caryopteris, forsythia, fuchsia and hydrangea are particularly sucsceptible.

Lacebugs also feed on sap. The **pieris lacebug** produces a silvery mottling on the upper surface and brown spots underneath the leaf. **Privet thrips** can produce similar silvering on privet (*Ligustrum*) and lilac (*Syringa*). The damage is mostly cosmetic but the bugs can be controlled by spraying with systemic or contact insecticides when damage is first noticed.

Tiny insects known as **psyllids**, together with their larvae known as

SOOTY MOULD

Sooty mould, shown here on camellia, develops as olive-green or black, powdery patches.

Sap-sucking insects feed by tapping into the plant's food-conducting vessels. The sap is rich in sugars and the insects often absorb far more than they need in order to obtain sufficient quantities of other nutrients. This excess sugar is excreted as honeydew, which falls on the leaves or ground below. Honeydew is very sticky and should be washed off regularly as it is likely to attract sooty mould – a powdery, black fungus that can quickly spread over leaves. Sooty mould does not harm plants directly but can grow thickly enough to interfere with photosynthesis by blocking out the light. Once the insects have been dealt with, the sooty mould should gradually wear away, or can be removed by sponging with water.

Viburnum whiteflies are tiny, moth-like insects. The larvae and pupae are immobile and scale-like, clustered on leaf undersides.

Young cushion scales look very like soft scales, but mature females produce conspicuous, white egg sacs, up to 1.5cm (½in) long.

Soft scales are flattened, and can grow up to 5mm (¼in) long. They vary in colour but are usually darker in the centre and paler round the edge.

The sap-sucking activities of the **pieris lacebug** create silvering on the upper surface and brown spots on the underside of pieris and rhododendron leaves.

Privet thrips are small, narrow insects that feed underneath the leaves and create silvery areas on the upper surface.

Box sucker damage can be identified by miniature 'cabbages' at the ends of shoots.

Capsid bug damage shows as irregular holes on young leaves such as those of hydrangea.

suckers, can cause distortion through their sap-sucking activities. **Box suckers** (see p91) feed at shoot tips, causing the leaves to curve inwards like miniature cabbages. **Bay sucker** feeds on leaf edges, which turn yellow, thicken and curl over. Suckers also produce honeydew, which may then attract **sooty mould** (see p90). Picking off affected leaves may be enough to control them; otherwise spray with a suitable systemic insecticide.

 Cushion scale (see p91) favours evergreen shrubs and climbers such as camellia, euonymus, rhododendron,

Deal with problems promptly to maintain attractive displays.

holly (*Ilex*), ivy (*Hedera*) and star jasmine (*Trachelospermum*). **Oleander scale**, which looks like a miniature fried egg, attacks many plants such as oleander (*Nerium*) and palms grown under cover in cool climates, and moves with them outdoors in warmer areas. Inconspicuous **soft scales** (see p91) live on the undersides of leaves, generally clustered near the veins, and often go unnoticed until sooty mould appears on the surface of the leaves below, feeding on the honeydew the scale insects have excreted. They attack a very wide range of plants, indoors and out. Generally scale insects do not do a great deal of damage, but the sooty mould they attract can be unsightly. In large numbers, they can weaken plants and depress flowering and fruiting. For treatment advice see p42.

Whitefly may be found on a few shrubs including *Viburnum tinus* (see p91) and honeysuckle (*Lonicera*). These are not the same as glasshouse whitefly or brassica whitefly. If they become a nuisance, spray with an appropriate insecticide.

GALL-FORMING PESTS

In response to egg-laying by tiny wasps or sap sucking by even tinier mites, many plants produce galls. Oak trees produce **spangle galls** and **silk button galls**, while lime trees are prone to **nail galls. Walnut blister mites** feed on leaf undersides, producing pale swellings. There is no effective treatment for any of these galls. If thought disfiguring, small numbers of galls can be cut out or picked off, but they are usually too widespread to make this feasible, and there is no practical way to prevent them. The damage is insignificant to the overall health of affected plants.

93

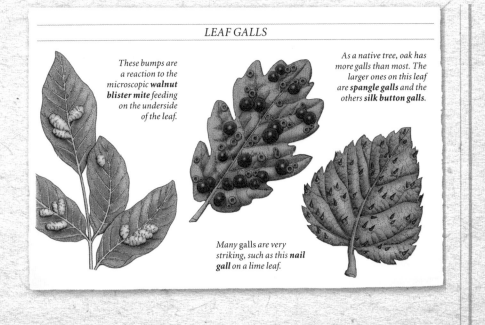

LEAF GALLS

*These bumps are a reaction to the microscopic **walnut blister mite** feeding on the underside of the leaf.*

*As a native tree, oak has more galls than most. The larger ones on this leaf are **spangle galls** and the others **silk button galls**.*

*Many galls are very striking, such as this **nail gall** on a lime leaf.*

DISTORTION CAUSED BY DISEASES

Azalea galls
*are large, pale
and dramatic.*

*Brown spots
and curled
leaves on
willow
indicate the
fungus disease
anthracnose.*

LEAF DISEASES CAUSING DISTORTION

A few fungi can produce significant distortion as well as the more usual discoloration. **Powdery mildew** (see p47) is one of these. Willow **anthracnose** develops as small, brown spots on twisted leaves, which fall early. Stem cankers may also appear, but there is no effective treatment for the disease, which trees seem able to live with, and is worse some years than others.

Azalea gall is very eye-catching, creating large, pale, swollen pouches on azaleas, which are often larger than the leaf they are growing on. White fungal spores then develop on the surface. There is no treatment other than picking off affected leaves, ideally before the spores develop.

LEAF DISEASES CAUSING SPOTS, STREAKS AND BLOTCHES

When trees and shrubs are being grown for ornamental purposes rather than, say, to produce fruit or timber, then a certain amount of damage to foliage should be tolerated. Spots, streaks and blotches may look unsightly but, even if many leaves are affected, the plant's overall health is unlikely to be compromised unless it is very young or already suffering from other problems. Improving the plant's growing conditions will help stave off trouble and, coupled with the impracticality of hand picking or spraying large shrubs and trees, is often the only practical way to help the plant deal with attacks when they occur.

Acer tar spot (see p96) is one of the most dramatic leaf spot diseases. It

NON-FLOWERING
AND NON-BERRYING SHRUBS

Control leafhoppers to keep rhododendrons blooming.

Rhododendron bud blast turns buds dark brown, and produces black, bristly fruiting bodies.

Rhododendron leafhoppers are 8–9mm (⅓–⅜in) long and turquoise-green with two orange stripes.

There can be a variety of reasons why otherwise healthy shrubs fail to flower, or flower but fail to produce fruit. Often, the plant is simply too young. Many shrubs don't flower until they are three or four years old and even if young plants are in flower when purchased they may revert to non-flowering for a couple of years while they settle in. Trees such as magnolias may not flower for 20 years or more. Lack of flowers can also be caused by incorrect pruning; very briefly, shrubs that flower in spring should be pruned in summer, and those flowering in summer should be pruned in winter or early spring. Pruning at other times can remove the flower buds.

Flower buds can also be destroyed by the weather. Late frosts can kill developing buds on, for example, hydrangea while summer drought can prevent the formation of buds on camellias. Sometimes, pests will take flower buds, but it is unlikely that they will denude the whole plant, though severe aphid infestation can prevent any flower buds opening on affected shrubs. Occasionally, diseases are responsible. One of these is **rhododendron bud blast,** which enters buds through damage caused by the **rhododendron leafhopper**. Spraying plants from early August with an appropriate insecticide should help control the leafhoppers and hence the occurrence of the disease.

If shrubs flower but do not berry, then late frost may be the problem, but it is more likely that the plant produces male and female flowers on different bushes, and both are needed to produce fruit. This is a common problem with hollies, but also applies to skimmia and *Viburnum davidii*.

affects sycamore and other maples, but will not spread to other types of plant. The disease overwinters as spores on fallen leaves, so where feasible, raking these up and burning or binning them should limit the spread of the disease.

TREE AND SHRUB DISEASES

Rust diseases, here on hypericum, can be identified by raised, powdery spots, in white, yellow, orange, brown or black, on the undersides of leaves.

Powdery mildew begins as white or grey, more or less circular patches, but can soon cover leaves completely. Young leaves often become distorted.

Yellow or white blotches, mottling or banding along the veins are symptoms of **virus** diseases.

Large, circular, inky black spots, each with a yellow halo, indicate infection with **acer tar spot**.

Box blight can start as dark brown spots appearing on the leaves in autumn or winter.

Box blight can be caused by two different fungi. The most serious is infection by cylindrocladium, which begins as spots on the leaves and dark streaks on the stems. Patches of grey-white fungal growth can appear in damp weather. The leaves turn brown and fall, and plants die back. The other fungus, volutella, produces masses of pink spores on the undersides of leaves, which then turn brown and drop off. Box blight caused by cylindrocladium particularly affects dwarf box (*Buxus sempervirens* 'Suffruticosa'), hedging and topiary, probably because air movement is restricted. They spread rapidly and there is no effective chemical treatment. Dig up and dispose of affected plants, including fallen leaves, ideally in dry weather to minimise the spread of spores. If replanting, consider alternatives such as box-leaved holly (*Ilex crenata*) or shrubby germander (*Teucrium fruticans*) for dwarf hedging, and yew (*Taxus*) for taller hedging or topiary.

Powdery mildew can affect many shrubs and trees, especially when stressed by dryness at the roots. Typical symptoms start with circular, white spots that join up to form irregular patches or even cover the whole leaf. This is often seen in young oaks and field maple (*Acer campestre*). Leaves of other affected shrubs, such as cotinus, can become distorted. With **rhododendron powdery mildew**, the symptoms are different, appearing as yellow blotches on the upper surface and pale brown, felty patches below. On cherry laurel (*Prunus laurocerasus*), yellow spots turn brown and the dead tissue falls away creating a shothole effect (see p155). If spotted early, attacks can be controlled by picking off badly affected leaves and spraying the remainder with a suitable fungicide. Otherwise, cut out badly damaged shoots in autumn.

Rusts can affect many trees and shrubs but individual rust species tend to affect only small groups of related plants: for example, **hypericum rust** (see p96) attacks only hypericums. Picking off affected leaves promptly can help limit the spread of the disease but spraying with an appropriate fungicide is often needed for full control.

Many shrubs seem to live quite happily with a degree of **virus** infection, which may show itself as mottling or streaks on leaves or flowers. Viruses cannot be treated, however, so if the discoloration is serious, or plant growth becomes distorted or flowering reduced, then remove and dispose of the plant.

• CONIFERS •

Conifers attract a far smaller range of pests and diseases than broadleaved trees and shrubs, though they are susceptible to much the same root-rotting fungi including **honey fungus** (see p46) and **phytophthora** (see p47).

PESTS ON SHOOTS

Fir (*Abies*), larch (*Larix*), pine (*Pinus*) and spruce (*Picea*) can become infested with sap-sucking pests known as adelgids. **Spruce gall adelgids** stimulate the production of small, pineapple-shaped galls at the branch tips of Norway spruce (*Picea abies*). Little real harm is done. On other conifers, the adelgids secrete a white, waxy covering but seem to do little damage. On small

Conifers attract few pests and are often trouble free.

trees, you could spray the immature stages of all these insects in late winter.

Aphids (see p40) can sometimes cause premature needle drop, so spray with a suitable insecticide. **Cypress aphids** attack a number of conifers, especially Leyland cypress (× *Cuprocyparis leylandii*). They attract sooty mould (see p90), and shoots turn yellow then brown. Gradually cut out dead patches so new growth can fill in the affected areas. Spraying in early summer can help prevent trouble. **Conifer red spider mites** mostly attack spruce (especially *Picea albertiana* 'Conica') but can also affect juniper (*Juniperus*) and thuja. Pale mottling gives a yellow-brown effect, and the needles drop early. Spray repeatedly with a suitable pesticide.

DISEASES ON SHOOTS

Rust can affect the needles of fir, larch and spruce, forming pustules of yellow spores. Some defoliation may occur, but no control is needed. **Juniper rust** also affects pears (see p152). Some **pine rusts** can produce stem cankers with yellow spores. Cut back affected branches to 20cm (8in) beyond the cankers.

Thuja blight affects only western red cedar (*Thuja plicata*) and is mainly a problem in hedges. Remove affected shoots before the spore bodies develop.

BROWNING IN CONIFER HEDGES

Plants grown as hedges are generally under stress caused by close planting, which means roots have to struggle for enough water and nutrients, and the loss of resources each time the hedge is pruned. They can develop brown patches simply as a result of scorching by very hot or very cold conditions or by lack of moisture. Heavy pruning can also cause dead areas – most conifers will not reshoot if cut back into brown stems, beyond where the needles or scales are growing. Pests and diseases can also be responsible, and tend to have a more visible effect on hedges than on plants grown as individuals.

99

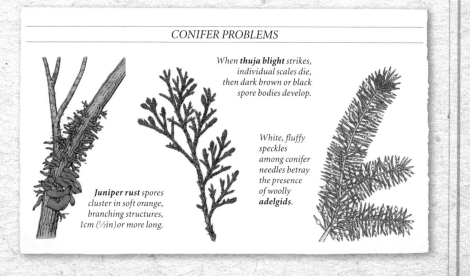

CONIFER PROBLEMS

When **thuja blight** strikes, individual scales die, then dark brown or black spore bodies develop.

Juniper rust spores cluster in soft orange, branching structures, 1cm (½in) or more long.

White, fluffy speckles among conifer needles betray the presence of woolly *adelgids*.

Modern rose-breeding programmes have developed varieties that are more robust, and less susceptible to common rose diseases, than earlier types. Unfortunately, pests can be as troublesome as ever.

LEAF PESTS

Large rose sawfly larvae can quickly strip foliage from affected bushes. In early summer, pick them off or spray with a suitable insecticide. Cut back badly affected shoots. The larvae of the rose slug sawfly, usually called **rose slugworm**, or rose skeletoniser, create pale patches by eating away the leaf surface. Control is not necessary.

A number of **moth caterpillars** feed on roses but rarely in such large numbers as

Choosing disease-resistant varieties will reduce problems with your roses.

to cause serious problems. Hand picking is usually enough, but wear gloves to handle hairy species. **Leaf-cutter bees** collect pieces of leaf to make their nests, which are cigar-shaped and created in holes made in the ground, chinks in walls and so on. The bees do seem to favour individual bushes, often roses, but the damage is insignificant and no action need be taken.

Capsid bugs (see p40) can also affect rose shoots. When the damage is spotted, the capsids have usually gone. Preventive spraying in late spring with a systemic insecticide can be worthwhile.

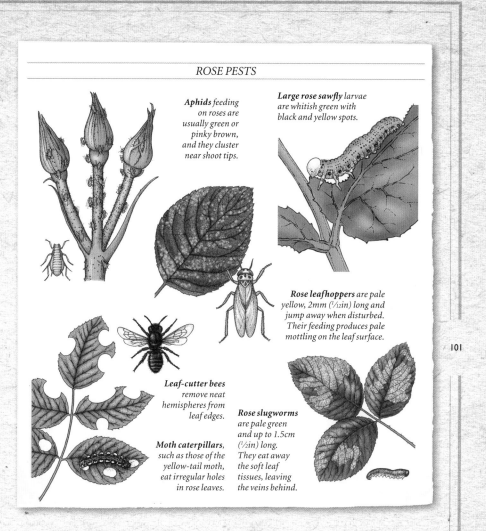

Aphids *feeding on roses are usually green or pinky brown, and they cluster near shoot tips.*

Large rose sawfly *larvae are whitish green with black and yellow spots.*

Rose leafhoppers *are pale yellow, 2mm (¹⁄₁₂in) long and jump away when disturbed. Their feeding produces pale mottling on the leaf surface.*

Leaf-cutter bees *remove neat hemispheres from leaf edges.*

Moth caterpillars, *such as those of the yellow-tail moth, eat irregular holes in rose leaves.*

Rose slugworms *are pale green and up to 1.5cm (½in) long. They eat away the soft leaf tissues, leaving the veins behind.*

101

Rose leafhoppers and **red spider mites** (see p42) can cause light-coloured mottling on the leaf surface which, if severe, can turn the whole leaf pale. Numbers can build up in hot weather and do damage out of proportion to their size. Control by spraying with a suitable pesticide.

PEST PROBLEMS CAUSING DISTORTION

Aphids deform young growth by clustering together on shoot tips and removing sap from the developing leaf and flower buds. Remove them before colonies build up.

Rose leaf-rolling sawfly lays its eggs then secretes chemicals that cause the leaf edges to roll down around them within 24 hours. The larvae hatch and continue to feed in the rolled-up leaves. Most attacks do not warrant any action, but the leaves can be picked off and disposed of.

LEAF DISEASES

The big three rose diseases are blackspot, powdery mildew and rust. All three are best tackled first by looking for resistant varieties, then by providing plants with good growing conditions to help them stave off attacks. If this is not sufficient, spray preventatively from spring, or as soon as a disease is spotted, with a suitable fungicide.

Blackspot often strikes early in the season and can defoliate plants almost as soon as flowering begins. It typically produces dark spots each with a yellow halo, then the leaves turn yellow and fall off. Even completely defoliated bushes manage to go on flowering and often leaf up well the following year, but the disease must weaken plants and the effects are unsightly. The spores

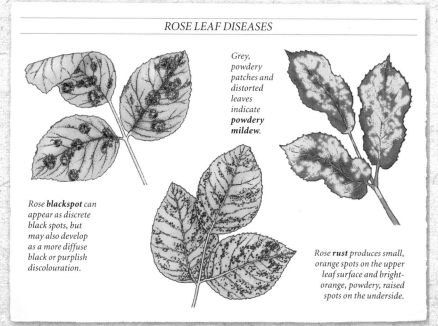

ROSE LEAF DISEASES

Grey, powdery patches and distorted leaves indicate **powdery mildew**.

Rose **blackspot** can appear as discrete black spots, but may also develop as a more diffuse black or purplish discolouration.

Rose **rust** produces small, orange spots on the upper leaf surface and bright-orange, powdery, raised spots on the underside.

VIRUSES AND MAGNESIUM DEFICIENCY

Viruses produce a range of leaf symptoms including yellow veining, mosaics, rings and spots. They rarely seem to affect the flowers or the plant's general growth. Viruses cannot be cured, so they must either be tolerated or the plants dug out and disposed of.

Roses are susceptible to magnesium deficiency, especially if grown on sandy soil or where there is an excess of potassium in the soil, which inhibits magnesium uptake. This also produces yellow areas, but these appear in a symmetrical way between the veins, and may then turn brown, while the veins remain green. Treat with foliar sprays of Epsom salts (magnesium sulphate) following the instructions on the packet.

Viruses usually produce yellow patterns on the leaves; this one follows the leaf veins.

*Yellow patches on leaves, with the veins remaining green, are symptoms of **magnesium deficiency**.*

overwinter partly on fallen foliage so it is worth clearing this up.

Rust tends to appear later than blackspot, but can also cause premature leaf loss. It may first appear as bright orange patches, up to 2.5cm (1in) long, on stems and leaf stalks, and affected shoots should be cut out. Later in the year, pustules of oranges spores appear on leaf undersides. The spores turn brown, then black and the leaves dry up and fall early. Spores overwinter partly on fallen leaves, so burn or bin these.

Powdery mildew can strike at any time, and can cause considerable damage by distorting shoot tips. It particularly attacks climbers trained on walls as these inevitably suffer from dryness at the roots. Shoots, leaves and flowers can be affected. The fungus shows on stems over winter as a grey, felt-like growth. Cut out affected shoots.

*Grey-brown, furry, fungal growth shows that the tissues have been invaded by **grey mould**.*

***Rose canker** browns and roughens the bark, and results in shoots dying back.*

STEM PROBLEMS

If stems start to die back, look for brown patches with small spots of rough bark. This is **rose canker**, which can generally be controlled by cutting out affected shoots. Be careful to cut back cleanly, just above a bud, without crushing or tearing the stem so that there is the minimum of damaged tissue for the fungus to reinvade. Sometimes, larger cankers develop at ground level, where the stem becomes swollen and the bark cracked and rough. These also need to be cut out. Where a rose has been planted too deeply, so that the graft union between stock and scion is buried, it should be lifted and replanted with the union just above ground level to make canker problems less likely.

If stems have blackened areas, and grey, fluffy growth develops, this indicates infection by **grey mould**. It usually appears when the stem has been damaged by something else, such as frost. Treat such problems by pruning back affected shoots well below the damaged area. Stems can also be affected by **powdery mildew** (see p103).

Sometimes roses produce healthy shoots that fail to develop any flowers. This is caused by damage to the tip, usually by **low temperatures**. Cut back these blind shoots, to encourage sideshoots to develop. Soft growth stimulated by too much nitrogen can be particularly prone to this problem, so do not overfeed rose plants.

Roses can also be affected by scale insects, which cluster on stems and can weaken plants by feeding on the sap. Two common ones are **brown scale** (see p160), with its domed, red-brown scales up to 6mm (¼in) across, and **scurfy scale**, with its flat, pale grey scales 2mm (¹⁄₁₂in) across. Scrub these insects off with a toothbrush and a little soapy water. Suitable pesticides can be applied to the more susceptible, juvenile stages in midsummer for brown scale and in early autumn for scurfy scale. Dead scales often remain attached to the stems, but new growth should be clear of them.

Roses need more care than many shrubs but are spectacular in bloom.

ROSE REPLANT DISEASE

If roses are planted in ground where roses were growing previously, they will often fail to thrive, remaining small and stunted with underdeveloped roots. This is known as rose sickness or rose replant disease and something similar occurs in other members of the rose family including apples, pears, plums and cherries. The cause is not entirely understood, and it is likely that a number of factors are involved. One is likely to be the soil-dwelling fungus pythium, which is known to attack roots, and another is soil-dwelling nematodes (eelworms) that carry plant viruses. Although these pathogens do not appear to affect established plants, the immature root systems of young plants cannot tolerate them. Depletion of nutrients by the previous plants is also likely to contribute to a poor performance. If affected plants are dug up, the roots cleaned and then planted elsewhere, they will often recover.

The easiest way to avoid replant disease is not to plant roses in the same place twice. However, if there is no alternative then improving the soil with substantial amounts of well-rotted manure has been shown to counteract the problem. Alternatively, when digging new planting holes, remove the soil to a depth of at least 30cm (1ft) and exchange it for soil in another part of the garden.

PROBLEMS WITH FLOWERS NOT OPENING

Sometimes, rose buds open as far as showing the petals, then the outer petals turn brown and stick together, preventing the bud opening further. This is called **capping** and is usually the result of bruising to the petals by heavy rain or hail. Cut off affected buds. In wet weather, opening flower buds can also become infected with **grey mould**, and this often follows capping. The buds rot and may develop a grey, furry covering. Remove and destroy them, to reduce the spread of the disease.

Pedicel necrosis, or death of the flower stalk, can happen if the bush is short of nutrients, or stressed by drought. The stem just behind the developing bud turns black and the bud dies. Cut back affected shoots and improve feeding and watering to overcome this problem.

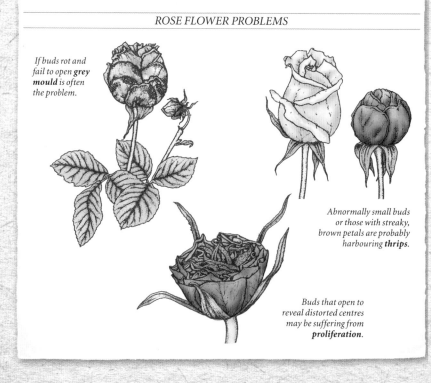

ROSE FLOWER PROBLEMS

If buds rot and fail to open grey mould is often the problem.

Abnormally small buds or those with streaky, brown petals are probably harbouring thrips.

Buds that open to reveal distorted centres may be suffering from proliferation.

DAMAGED FLOWERS

Flower buds and opening flowers may be nibbled by various **moth caterpillars**. If you can spot them, pick them off or spray badly affected plants with a suitable insecticide. Another flower-eating pest is the **rose chafer**, a striking, metallic-green beetle, up to 2cm (¾in) long. It is not worth trying to control these highly mobile beetles.

Thrips are thin, black or yellow insects, about 2mm (¹⁄₁₂in) long, which live in between the rose petals. They feed by removing sap, and this can lead to streaky petals or distorted blooms. Spraying with a suitable systemic insecticide will control thrips. In all cases, badly damaged buds should be removed, to encourage new growth.

With **proliferation**, the developing flower is distorted so that one or more small buds develop in the centre of a normal flower. These buds generally do not open. The cause is usually damage to the growing bud in the very early

107

Nip problems in the bud by checking your rose bushes regularly.

stages of development, either by insects or frosts. It is more common in old cabbage roses and bourbons than in modern hybrids. If the problem occurs repeatedly then the cause is more likely to be a virus and the plant should be destroyed.

VEGETABLES

• INTRODUCTION •

In this chapter on the problems gardeners are likely to come across when growing vegetables outdoors or under glass, the vegetables are arranged alphabetically, although related ones that suffer the same pests and diseases, such as the cabbage family (brassicas), are grouped together.

Most vegetables are routinely grown from seeds, and problems with seeds and seedlings are covered first. Problems with other growing methods, such as using sets (small bulbs) to start onions and tubers to start potatoes, are dealt with under the individual vegetables concerned.

• SEEDS & SEEDLINGS •

SOLVING VEGETABLE SEED PROBLEMS

General problems with seeds failing to grow are covered in ornamental seeds (see p52). Vegetable seeds vary enormously in size, from tiny celeriac to massive broad beans. Smaller seeds have far fewer reserves, which can make them more vulnerable to less-than-perfect growing conditions. Large seeds, on the other hand, are likely to be much more attractive to pests, such as mice.

Home-saved pea and bean seeds, particularly broad beans, may be damaged by **bean seed beetles**. Such beetles lay their eggs on the developing pods and the larvae tunnel into the seeds. When the seeds come to be planted they are marked by circular exit holes where the adult beetles have left. There is no practical way to control this

pest, and affected seeds will usually still grow into healthy plants.

SOLVING VEGETABLE SEEDLING PROBLEMS

To overcome general problems with seedlings refer to the detailed discussion in ornamental seedlings (p53).

Seedlings of brassicas, which include broccoli, Brussels sprouts, cabbages, cauliflowers, radishes, swedes and turnips, can suffer from a couple of specific problems. **Flea beetles** are shiny, black insects, 2mm (1/12in) long, which leap off plants when disturbed. Although they may be killed, seedlings usually grow through this phase, provided they are well watered. Keep flea beetles out with insect-proof mesh or, if necessary, treat with a systemic contact insecticide approved for use on brassicas. Flea beetles

SEEDLING PROBLEMS

*Attacks by **bean seed fly** maggots result in seedlings that are distorted or fail to grow.*

***Flea beetles** feed on brassicas, particularly seedlings, peppering the leaves with small holes.*

*If brassica seedlings with two to four leaves suddenly topple over, suspect **wirestem fungus**.*

*Young pea and broad bean plants may be attacked by **pea and bean weevils**. These grey-brown beetles, 3mm (⅛in) long, drop to the ground when disturbed.*

will also attack related ornamental plants including aubrieta, stocks (*Matthiola*) and wallflowers (*Erysimum*).

Brassica seedlings can be affected by **wirestem fungus**, too. This kills their roots, and causes the stems to shrink at ground level so the seedlings collapse. It cannot be treated, but sowing thinly into well-cultivated ground, or into pots of good-quality compost, and not overwatering will help avoid the problem.

Pea and broad bean seedlings can be attacked by **pea and bean weevils**. They cut semicircular notches from the leaf edges, and these are so regularly distributed that they look like the leaf's normal shape. The damage is not significant to the plant's development, and no action need be taken.

Runner and French beans are attacked by the **bean seed fly**. This lays its eggs on freshly planted seeds and its white maggots, up to 8mm (⅓in) long, feed on the cotyledons (seed leaves) and shoots. These are, therefore, unable to grow properly and may fail to appear at all. Protect seeds outdoors with insect-proof mesh, or start them off in pots under cover.

• ASPARAGUS •

Asparagus is not a fussy perennial provided the soil is well drained.

ENVIRONMENTAL PROBLEMS

Asparagus starts into growth in early to midspring, so can be caught by late **frosts**. Cut out damaged spears, as they will not recover. Prevent the problem by protecting beds with polythene or horticultural fleece supported on hoops.

PEST PROBLEMS

Young asparagus shoots are attractive to **slugs** and **snails** (see p43). **Asparagus beetle** attacks the foliage and surface tissue on asparagus stems. Pick off the beetles and their larvae or spray plants with a contact insecticide approved for use on asparagus. Also burn old stems at the end of the year.

DISEASE PROBLEMS

If plants become yellow and stunted, the roots may have been affected by **violet root rot**. This fungus produces resting bodies known as sclerotia, which can remain in the soil for long periods and affect other susceptible plants. If only a small part of the bed is affected, dig out the damaged plants and adjacent soil. Otherwise, remove all the plants and start again with fresh stock elsewhere.

ASPARAGUS PROBLEMS

*Jazzy **asparagus beetles** are easy to spot but hard to catch or spray as they drop to the ground when disturbed. The muddy green larvae are easier to deal with.*

Frost damage causes withering and bending of shoot tips. Severe frost may cause shoots to turn black.

Violet root rot can be identified by the purple, web-like strands that develop on asparagus roots.

These are prone to pests that thrive in high temperatures as well as to diseases that favour cool, damp conditions.

PEST PROBLEMS

Aubergines seem to act as a magnet for **glasshouse whitefly** (see p44). Always treat them before numbers build up. Sticky, yellow traps can catch some adults and act as a useful early warning device so you can start biological control measures or apply a suitable insecticide.

The feeding activities of **glasshouse red spider mites** (see p42) produce mottled leaves, and they also create areas of webbing. Increasing humidity will help control mite numbers, but they will also need treating with a suitable pesticide, or biological control.

Aphids (see p40) can damage growing tips and reduce flowering so check regularly and squash colonies or spray with a suitable insecticide. Biological control can also be used in glasshouses.

DISEASE PROBLEMS

Verticillium wilt attacks through the roots but the symptoms are most noticeable above ground as leaves turn yellow and all or part of the plant wilts. Remove affected plants and do not

> ### AUBERGINE PROBLEMS
>
> The symptoms of **verticillium wilt** can look like water shortage, because this disease blocks the water-carrying vessels in the plant's roots and stems.
>
> Fruit that rots on the plant and develops a grey-brown, furry fungus has been affected by **grey mould**.

113

replant in the same area. This wilt is largely soilborne, so growing plants in tubs of compost should avoid an attack, as should using tolerant varieties.

Grey mould can affect leaves, stems and fruits. Prompt removal of dead or dying leaves and improved ventilation will help minimise attacks.

Cucumber mosaic virus (see p124) causes yellow mottling on leaves and distorted growth. Destroy affected plants.

This section covers broad beans, French beans and runner beans. Although they can suffer from a wide range of problems, all three beans usually produce a good crop without too much intervention from the gardener.

ALL BEANS

Bean seed fly can attack seedlings at the point at which they start to grow (see p111), while **black bean aphids** can be a serious pest, particularly on broad beans. They also attack French and runner beans, dahlias, nasturtiums (*Tropaeolum*), guelder rose (*Viburnum opulus*) and mock orange (*Philadelphus*). These aphids cluster on shoot tips and also on the spine of developing pods leading to distortion and poor growth. Pinching out the tips of broad beans once the plants are in flower can remove a lot of pests but spraying with an insecticide approved for use on beans will give better control. On runner beans, only isolated shoots or leaves may be affected and these are easily picked off.

Bean rust affects all beans, and although different species of rust are involved the symptoms and treatment are the same. Rust spots tend to appear late in the season so they inflict only limited damage. Pick off the worst affected leaves and, at the end of the season, dispose of the plants and any fallen debris. Wider spacing to improve air circulation can reduce the incidence of bean rust.

Beans can also suffer from a variety of **fungal root and stem rots** that can lead to yellowing or wilting of leaves and sometimes blackening of stems and collapse of the whole plant. Remove

BEAN LEAF PROBLEMS

Halo blight infects French and runner beans, producing dark, angular spots with a pale halo.

Bean rust appears as dark, raised, powdery spots on the undersides of the leaves.

114

badly affected plants and do not grow beans in the same area for a few years. Some French and runner bean varieties are resistant to one common problem – fusarium wilt.

BROAD BEANS

Bean seed beetles (see p110) may eat holes in broad bean seeds, and young plants may be nibbled by **pea and bean weevils** (see p111).

Broad beans can also be affected by **chocolate spot**. In damp conditions, this fungus can spread rapidly, so the spots join up and the plant may turn black and die. Once the disease is established it cannot be controlled, so pull out the worst-affected plants. This will help any that remain by improving air circulation. In future, plant beans in well-drained soil, space them well apart and avoid high-nitrogen fertiliser, which produces soft, vulnerable growth especially on overwintered plants.

FRENCH AND RUNNER BEANS

These are easily damaged by **frost**, which produces brown patches on the leaves. Cover young plants with cloches if more frost is forecast. The main pests of French and runner beans are **slugs** and **snails**. They can devour young plants

TOO FEW PODS?

Sometimes, runner beans fail to set many pods, despite flowering well. A lack of moisture at root level is often the cause of this. Therefore, improve the moisture-holding capacity of the soil where beans are to grow by adding plenty of bulky organic material, and sow white-flowered varieties, which are more drought-tolerant. Lack of pollinating insects can be a problem in very cold or windy weather, when bees are reluctant to fly. Some bumblebees also 'cheat' by biting into the back of the flower to take the nectar without collecting or depositing any pollen. There isn't really anything you can do about this, although you can grow climbing French beans instead, which are self-fertile.

overnight, and continue to feed on the leaves, flowers and pods of those that survive. Snails, in particular, can quite easily scale climbing bean supports. For control measures see p43.

Bean foliage can be affected by **halo blight**, a bacterial infection that can result in whole leaves turning yellow and dying. This reduces overall growth and yield. Remove affected leaves promptly. Dispose of diseased plants at the end of the season by burning or binning, and do not save seed from them. Look out for resistant varieties if halo blight is a regular problem.

Brassicas are a large and important group, which includes broccoli, Brussels sprouts, cabbages, calabrese, cauliflowers, Chinese cabbages, kale, kohlrabi, pak choi, radishes, rocket, swedes and turnips. Unfortunately, brassicas are also a magnet for pests and diseases and it's a lucky gardener who doesn't have any problems when growing them. Most brassicas are ultimately derived from the wild cabbage found on the Atlantic seaboard of Europe and are mainly hardy, while some varieties of broccoli, calabrese, cauliflower and Chinese cabbage are frost-sensitive. Compared with other vegetables, brassicas are relatively slow-growing, occupying the same ground for a long period, so good preparation, including the addition of plenty of soil nutrients, pays dividends.

SEEDLINGS

Brassicas are usually started off in a seedbed and only moved to their final positions when they have four to six leaves. Seedlings can be killed by **wirestem fungus** (see p111) or annihilated by **slugs** (see p43) and **flea beetles** (see p110). One way to overcome such problems is to start plants off indoors in pots so they are better able to fend for themselves when planted out.

SMALL LEAF PESTS

Cabbage whitefly attacks brassicas and, occasionally, broad beans. These pests do little direct damage, but excrete large amounts of honeydew, which in turn attracts sooty mould that can make the leaves unpleasant. Attacks can be tolerated, and the effects washed off, or they can be treated with an insecticide suitable for use on brassicas.

Heavy attacks of **mealy cabbage aphid** can distort and damage young plants and should be treated by

Netting or mesh will exclude birds and butterflies from brassica crops.

116

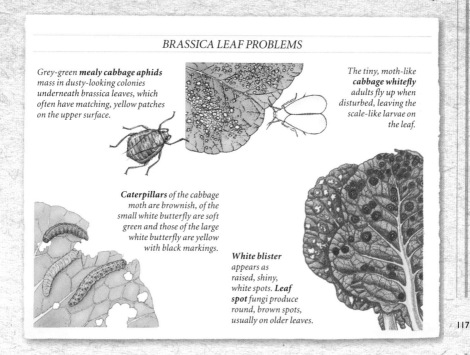

*Grey-green **mealy cabbage aphids** mass in dusty-looking colonies underneath brassica leaves, which often have matching, yellow patches on the upper surface.*

*The tiny, moth-like **cabbage whitefly** adults fly up when disturbed, leaving the scale-like larvae on the leaf.*

***Caterpillars** of the cabbage moth are brownish, of the small white butterfly are soft green and those of the large white butterfly are yellow with black markings.*

***White blister** appears as raised, shiny, white spots. **Leaf spot** fungi produce round, brown spots, usually on older leaves.*

squashing or spraying with a suitable insecticide. Colonies on older leaves can generally be tolerated.

LARGE LEAF PESTS

Caterpillars are often the most problematic insect pest of brassicas because they can do considerable damage quite quickly and often eat their way into the centre of the developing plant, where they are hard to tackle. Hand picking can be effective on small plants, but spraying will often be necessary to control caterpillars once they become established on larger plants. The best approach is to keep adult butterflies and moths well away from plants, using insect-proof mesh.

Pigeons can also do serious damage to brassicas, especially in winter when plants can be completely stripped. Protect plants with netting, as bird-scaring devices are rarely effective.

LEAF DISEASES

White blister is a fungal-like disease that affects brassicas and a few other related plants including honesty (*Lunaria*) and the weed shepherd's purse (*Capsella bursa-pastoris*). Plants often look as

Aim to prevent problems, or treat them early, to produce a healthy crop.

the plants wilting. Young plants are often killed though older ones may survive provided they have plenty of moisture. Prevent root fly attacks by fitting cabbage collars – flat discs of old carpet, roofing felt or similar – around the plant stems so these flies cannot reach the soil. Alternatively,

though they have been splashed with white paint, but, in fact, the disease does little damage and affected plants can still be eaten. Removing badly affected leaves, and thinning plants out, can help reduce the spread of white blister, and some resistant varieties are available.

ROOT PESTS

Damage to roots can be more devastating than attacks on leaves because it usually goes unnoticed until well advanced, and once the roots are badly damaged it is very difficult for them to recover. Consequently, prevention is by far the best way to deal with root pests and diseases.

Cabbage root flies lay their eggs in the soil adjacent to brassica plants and the larvae then hatch out and attack the roots. Often the first sign of damage is

CROPPING PROBLEMS

Mature cabbages sometimes fail to develop a firm, solid heart. This is generally as a result of poor soil conditions – insufficient organic material or moisture – or poor planting techniques, so plants do not have their roots firmed well into the soil. Sometimes, a good heart is developed but then splits. This may be caused by frost, but can also be triggered by a long period of dry conditions followed by heavy rain or irrigation. Cauliflowers sometimes fail to develop full-sized curds, and this is generally due to an erratic water supply. Frost can also damage well-grown curds, turning them brown. Good cultivation is the best way of avoiding all these problems.

cover plants with insect-proof mesh, which will also keep out many other pests. Avoid growing brassicas in the same position the following year.

Turnip gall weevils can affect all brassicas. The galls produced on the roots can look like club root (see below) but if cut open they are hollow and often contain a gall weevil grub. Galls do not have much effect on the function of the roots, so are not really a problem on leafy vegetables, but the distortion can be a nuisance on turnips and swedes. There is no practical treatment.

ROOT DISEASES

Club root is the most serious disease of brassicas, and can kill young plants, though older plants often survive. It is usually noticed when plants turn yellow and wilt; if pulled up, any swollen roots will confirm the identity of this disease. Wallflowers (*Erysimum*), stocks (*Matthiola*) and some related weeds are also susceptible. Club root is caused by a slime mould that can survive in the soil for 20 years or more, even with no plants to infect. It is usually brought into gardens on infected plants or by infected soil on boots or tools. There is no chemical treatment available, so affected plants should be pulled up and

BRASSICA ROOT PROBLEMS

Cabbage root fly maggots eat all the small roots then bore into the taproot.

Turnip gall weevils stimulate the growth of round, hollow nodules, often containing a maggot.

Swollen, distorted roots betray the presence of **club root**.

disposed of. Wet, acidic soils favour the pathogen, so improving drainage and liming the soil should reduce attacks. Another line of defence is to start plants off in pots of compost so they can develop a substantial root system before being planted out. There are also a few resistant varieties available.

CARROT PROBLEMS

*Stunted foliage with yellow banding and a red flush are symptoms of **motley dwarf disease** in carrots.*

*Long **splits** can look dramatic but the roots are still edible, though they do not store well.*

120

However, it can also be a symptom of carrot fly or viral attack (see below).

Carrot roots **fork** as a result of damage to the growing tip and they **split** lengthways if water supplies are erratic. Overcrowding can contribute to both these problems. Reduce problems by growing round or stump-rooted varieties on stony soil, by sowing seeds direct in their final positions, and by thinning where necessary.

PEST PROBLEMS

Carrot fly attacks carrots, parsley, parsnips and celery. These small, dark flies lay their eggs in the soil near the carrots. Maggots feed on the fine roots, which can lead to reddened foliage, and then tunnel into the main root. To prevent damage, erect a barrier to exclude the female flies (see p30). A covering of fleece also works well early in the season, but is too warm in the summer, so use insect-proof mesh instead.

DISEASE PROBLEMS

Carrots can suffer **violet root rot** (see p112). A combination of viruses causes carrot **motley dwarf disease**, in which roots fail to develop properly. Dispose of affected plants. It also affects parsley.

Carrots are pretty resilient and, carrot fly apart, are easy and reliable croppers.

ENVIRONMENTAL PROBLEMS

Carrots under stress from a **sudden cold snap** or **shortage of water** tend to develop red-tinged foliage. This should disappear when the cause is rectified.

• CELERY & CELERIAC •

Celery needs stable growing conditions and a steady water supply to thrive, while celeriac is more tolerant of dry conditions.

ENVIRONMENTAL PROBLEMS

If celery is **chilled** or **short of water** it bolts (runs to seed), which adversely affects the quality and quantity of its leaf stalks. Lack of water can also cause vertical stem cracks. Celery is also prone to a **lack of boron**, which causes horizontal, brown cracks across the stems, poor growth and yellowing leaves. Prevent this by adding borax (sodium tetraborate) to the soil before planting.

PEST PROBLEMS

Slug damage encourages rotting fungi (see p43). **Celery leaf miner** tunnels into leaves, thereby checking growth and producing unpalatable heads. They also attack celeriac, parsnip and lovage. Use insect-proof mesh to minimise attacks.

DISEASE PROBLEMS

Celery leaf spot appears as small, brown spots with pinpoint, black fruiting bodies. Prevent by spraying with the appropriate fungicide. Destroy plants affected by **mosaic viruses**. Celery can also be affected by **violet root rot** (see p112).

CELERY AND CELERIAC PROBLEMS

Celery leaf miners create irregular, pale green blotches, which then dry out and turn brown.

*Celery needs well-watered soil, which inevitably attracts **slugs**.*

Mosaic viruses such as cucumber mosaic and arabis mosaic virus cause yellow mottling and distortion.

• CHARD & BEETROOT •

Chard, which is also known as leaf beet, leaf chard, Swiss chard, perpetual spinach and spinach beet, is a very easy and productive crop to grow. Beetroot is also fairly trouble free.

ENVIRONMENTAL PROBLEMS

If beetroot suffers a check to growth caused by overcrowding or lack of soil moisture it may **bolt**. This inhibits the storage of food in the root, and no useful crop is produced. In future, add well-rotted organic matter to improve the soil's moisture-holding ability, water in dry periods and look out for bolt-resistant varieties. Chard is much less likely to bolt than closely related spinach.

PEST PROBLEMS

Once they are past the seedling stage, chard and beetroot do not seem very attractive to **slugs** (see p43), which may nibble a few holes in the leaves but rarely seem to do significant damage. If seedlings regularly disappear, start seeds off in pots and plant out as young plants.

    Leaf miner activity can check the growth of young plants so crush maggots inside the leaves at once. The damage to established plants is not usually severe enough to warrant any action.

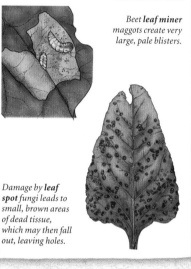

CHARD AND BEET PROBLEMS

Beet **leaf miner** maggots create very large, pale blisters.

Damage by **leaf spot** fungi leads to small, brown areas of dead tissue, which may then fall out, leaving holes.

DISEASE PROBLEMS

Leaf spot diseases can be controlled by removing badly affected leaves, thinning out plants that are growing too close together and destroying plants at the end of the season. Grow beetroot and related plants in a different area to help reduce carry-over of the disease.

    Chard, and some varieties of beetroot, grown at very close spacing for cut-and-come again salad leaves, can in cold, damp weather succumb to diseases such as **downy mildew** (see p45) and **grey mould** (see p45). If grown indoors, improve ventilation.

122

• CUCURBITS •

Cucurbits are the cucumber family, which includes courgettes, marrows, melons, pumpkins and squashes. Many have tropical or subtropical origins, so need a long, warm growing season, at least some of which should be in a heated glasshouses in cooler climates. This can make them prone to high-temperature pests, while growing outdoors they are susceptible to low-temperature diseases.

PEST PROBLEMS INDOORS

Cucumbers are particularly prone to **glasshouse red spider mite** (see p42), which produces fine, pale mottling on the foliage. Webs appear, particularly between the leaf blade and leaf stalk. When numbers build up, red spider mites stop plants growing and often kill them as heavy infestations are very difficult to control. **Glasshouse whitefly** are easier to spot in the early stages, and are less damaging overall, but still a nuisance (see p41).

PEST PROBLEMS OUTDOORS

All cucurbits are attractive to **slugs** and **snails** (see p43), especially young plants, flowers and young fruits. **Aphids** (see p40) spread viral diseases, so control them with a suitable contact insecticide.

DISEASE PROBLEMS INDOORS

Cucumber mosaic virus is usually spread by aphids, but can also be transferred after handling affected plants so always wash your hands thoroughly afterwards. Any fruit that develop will be blotched, deformed and

FRUITING PROBLEMS

Although cucurbits produce separate male and female flowers on the same plant, most modern varieties of cucumber have been selected to produce only female flowers. These can be identified by the miniature fruit behind the petals, and they form fruit without being pollinated. Cucumber fruits may turn bitter if plants suffer from poor growing conditions or an excess of nitrogen.

With courgettes, marrows, pumpkins and squashes, female flowers do need to be pollinated to produce fruit. This is usually done by bees, and fruit may not develop if cold or wet weather prevents them flying. To hand pollinate, shake a male flower to release pollen over the centre of the female flower.

If developing fruit turns yellow then drops off, it most probably was not properly pollinated, or the plant is not able to carry the number of fruit that have set. If the majority of fruit fail to develop, the plant is likely to be short of food or water.

inedible. Destroy infected plants as soon as problems are spotted. In future, look for resistant varieties.

Grey mould attacks fruit that has been damaged in any way or is simply not growing strongly. Good ventilation, heating when needed and prompt removal of dead flowers, damaged leaves or fruit will minimise the incidence.

Powdery mildew is most likely to attack when plants are stressed through shortage of moisture at the roots. This disease can be fatal if it attacks early in the season, and there are no fungicides available to control powdery mildew on curcubits.

DISEASE PROBLEMS OUTDOORS

Cucumber mosaic virus, grey mould and powdery mildew can also occur outdoors. Protect fruit lying on the ground from rot by lifting it onto a tile or small paving slab. Powdery mildew almost inevitably strikes towards the end of the season, and badly affected plants should be pulled up.

In **stem, foot and root rots** a variety of fungi are involved, attacking young plants at or near soil level, and usually killing them. Reduce the risk of infection by not planting out too soon and by not growing cucurbits in the same piece of ground each year.

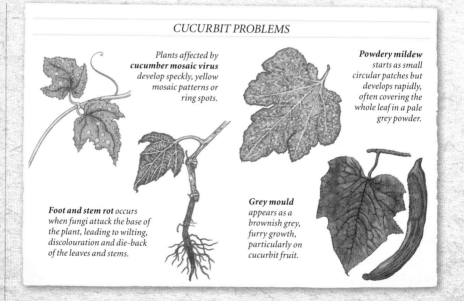

CUCURBIT PROBLEMS

Plants affected by **cucumber mosaic virus** develop speckly, yellow mosaic patterns or ring spots.

Powdery mildew starts as small circular patches but develops rapidly, often covering the whole leaf in a pale grey powder.

Foot and stem rot occurs when fungi attack the base of the plant, leading to wilting, discolouration and die-back of the leaves and stems.

Grey mould appears as a brownish grey, furry growth, particularly on cucurbit fruit.

124

• CULINARY HERBS •

Culinary herbs come from many different plant families, and originate in a range of climates. They also live for varying lengths of time. This makes it difficult to generalise about their pests and diseases, but herbs are often trouble free and rarely need serious intervention by the gardener.

ENVIRONMENTAL PROBLEMS

Most Mediterranean herbs, including bay, marjoram, rosemary, sage, tarragon and thyme, prefer well-drained soil and plenty of sunshine. Some are rather tender and can be damaged by severe **frost**, but far more plants are killed by **wet soil over winter** than by low temperatures. Avoid these problems by improving soil drainage – which can be achieved by digging in plenty of grit – or growing herbs in containers. Taking cuttings in late summer is a useful insurance, especially as many of these shrubby herbs are relatively short-lived – even in good growing conditions.

Herbs that need comparatively moist conditions, such as mint, coriander and lovage, can **bolt** or develop **unpleasant flavours** in hot, dry conditions. Avoid this by growing them in a shady area or, for annuals, at cooler times of year.

GENERAL PEST PROBLEMS

Slugs are a particular menace to basil, but can also do significant damage to parsley and other soft herbs, and even to woody herbs, by devouring all the new spring growth. Protect plants by scattering slug pellets or powders, hand picking or trapping slugs, or treating the soil with parasitic nematodes (see p43).

Leafhoppers suck sap and these tiny insects fly up when disturbed. They can do significant damage, especially in hot weather when numbers build up. Their feeding activities lead to pale speckling or silvering of the leaves and reduced growth. Treat leafhoppers with an insecticide approved for use on edible herbs.

PEST PROBLEMS ON SPECIFIC HERBS

Rosemary beetle, and its larvae, feed on rosemary, lavender, sage and thyme, and the damage is most noticeable in autumn and spring. A few insects can be tolerated, but if damage is severe either hand pick by shaking the beetles onto newspaper or a white cloth on the ground, or treat with an insecticide suitable for use on edible herbs. **Mint beetles**, which are metallic green, attack

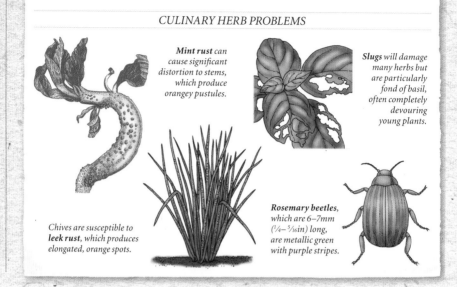

Mint rust can cause significant distortion to stems, which produce orangey pustules.

Slugs will damage many herbs but are particularly fond of basil, often completely devouring young plants.

Chives are susceptible to **leek rust**, which produces elongated, orange spots.

Rosemary beetles, which are 6–7mm (¼–⁵⁄₁₆in) long, are metallic green with purple stripes.

126

only mint, and rarely do enough damage to require treatment.

Bay trees can be troubled by **bay sucker**, which causes the leaf edges to thicken, turn yellow and roll under, and by **soft scale** – a scale insect that lives underneath the leaves, sucking sap and excreting honeydew, which attracts sooty mould (see p90).

Parsley is susceptible to **carrot fly** (see p120) and **celery leaf miners** (see p121).

DISEASE PROBLEMS ON SPECIFIC HERBS

Both chives and mint can suffer from rust. **Mint rust** can also affect marjoram and savory. Young stems can become distorted, with yellow flecks. Orangey, raised spots appear on leaves and stems, later turning dark brown. Always remove infected plants promptly, including any debris, and replant fresh stock on a different site.

Chives are susceptible to **leek rust**, which also affects garlic, onions and other alliums. It appears as elongated powdery spots, often around the time that the chives flower. Treat by cutting back and destroying all the foliage. Regrowth may also be infected, but if this is also cut back the next flush of foliage should be clear. If this fails, dig the plants up and start again with new plants on fresh ground.

• LEEKS •

Leeks originate in central Asia and are one of our hardiest vegetables.

ENVIRONMENTAL PROBLEMS

Overwintered leeks may start to **flower** in spring, especially if the soil becomes dry. Avoid the problem by harvesting leeks at their peak. If you want leeks to use in spring, choose a late-maturing variety.

PEST PROBLEMS

Leek moth caterpillars and **allium leaf miners** (which are the larvae of a small fly) feed by tunnelling between the upper and lower leaf surfaces. Later, they bore into the shaft where the leaf miners pupate. The moth caterpillars re-emerge to pupate on the leaves, so the pupae can be picked off. The pest damage may not be that serious but it lets in fungal rots that can destroy the crop. Protect plants from the start using insect-proof mesh. There are no suitable insecticides for either pest.

Leeks are also attractive to **onion thrips** (see p129) and **onion fly** (see p130).

DISEASE PROBLEMS

Leek rust tends to develop during long periods of wet weather, but it affects the overall crop only marginally. Disposing of all crop debris and growing leeks, onions and garlic in a different area each year should help reduce problems.

Leeks can also suffer from **onion white rot** (see p130).

LEEK PROBLEMS

Allium leaf miner larvae grow up to 4mm (⅛in) long, produce linear tunnels and turn into dark brown pupae in the shaft of the leek.

Leek moth caterpillars, up to 12mm (½in) long, cause blotchy patches and pupate in silk cocoons.

Leek rust can be identified by yellow or orange, powdery spot on the leaves.

Warm, not hot, temperatures and a steady moisture supply suit lettuces.

ENVIRONMENTAL PROBLEMS

In hot weather sow seeds into moist soil in the evening so high temperatures do not inhibit germination, and keep plants well watered to avoid **bolting**.

PEST PROBLEMS

Slugs and **snails** love lettuce. Growing plants to a reasonable size in containers before planting out helps improve their chances, but further pest control may be required (see p43).

Cutworms eat taproots and the base of stems, often causing plants to collapse. Search the soil near affected plants to find the culprits.

Plants affected by **lettuce root aphids** grow slowly and wilt in hot weather. These aphids cover themselves with white, waxy flakes and also excrete honeydew, which may attract ants. In future, cover lettuce plants with insect-proof mesh, or use resistant varieties.

DISEASE PROBLEMS

Lettuce downy mildew attacks old leaves first, which turn yellow and develop off-white fungal growth. **Grey mould** (see p45) often produces grey-brown fungal growth. Remove affected leaves on older plants and improve air flow.

LETTUCE PROBLEMS

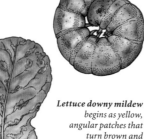

Cutworms *are the large, dirty brown caterpillars of a number of moths. They eat at night and curl up when resting during the daytime.*

Lettuce downy mildew *begins as yellow, angular patches that turn brown and papery or soft.*

Lettuce root aphids *are pale yellow and feed underground on plant roots.*

• ONIONS, SHALLOTS & GARLIC •

Onions have evolved from a group of wild ancestors in central Asia, with its bitterly cold winters and scorching hot summers, where they grow in stony areas with little competition from other plants. It is still true today that onions dislike weed competition and need a good, hot summer to ripen, so that they will store well. Despite being potentially prone to lots of problems, onions, shallots and garlic are relatively trouble free to cultivate.

Onions, shallots and garlic are generally easy to grow and produce a high yield.

ENVIRONMENTAL PROBLEMS

Onions tend to **bolt** if they suffer drought at a critical period. Bolting can also be caused by sowing seeds or planting sets too early, or in cold weather. If **flower stems** appear, cut them off but leave the bulbs to mature. Use these first as they do not store well. Drought followed by heavy rain can cause onion bulbs to **split**. Although perfectly usable, they may rot if stored. Too much manure or nitrogen in the soil or prolonged wet weather can lead to the development of an abnormally thick neck. Such **bull-necked onions** also store poorly. By providing good growing conditions, you will overcome all these problems.

PROBLEMS WITH ONION SETS

Onions can be grown from seed, but it is quicker and easier to start with small onions, known as sets. Push these into well-prepared soil, with the tops still showing. Keep **birds** and rodents such as **mice** and **voles** away from the sets until they are well rooted, by covering them with fleece or netting.

LEAF PESTS

Onion thrips are tiny, narrow, sap-sucking insects whose activities cause silvery white speckling on leaves. If young plants are severely attacked they can be permanently damaged, so treat thrips with an insecticide suitable for onions. Otherwise they can be tolerated, or excluded with insect-proof mesh.

Onion **eelworms** are microscopic nematodes that invade young plants from the soil. Affected plants become distorted, bloated and soft. Young plants generally die. Older, infested plants may survive and produce bulbs, but these tend to rot if stored. There is no chemical treatment for onion eelworms, which survive in the soil for several years. Many other vegetables act as carriers without suffering symptoms and allow the eelworms to increase. Brassicas and lettuce are not affected, so plant these for a couple of years where onion eelworm has been a problem before planting onions again.

Allium leaf miners and **leek moths** (see p127) can attack onions and shallots.

LEAF DISEASES

Downy mildew attacks usually start in the upper part of the leaves. The disease is worse in wet weather, and the earlier in the season it occurs the poorer the resulting crop. There is no fungicide treatment, but removing diseased leaves promptly may save plants and prevent the spores from affecting the bulbs. Onions and garlic are also susceptible to **leek rust** (see p127).

BULB PESTS

Onion fly lays its eggs on or near onion plants, and the larvae feed for a few weeks before pupating in the soil. The damage can kill young plants, and spoil older ones by allowing in fungal rots. If plants collapse, check for the maggots and destroy them before they have a chance to pupate. Onions suffer most from attacks by onion fly, but shallots, garlic and leeks can also be targeted. There are no pesticides suitable for controlling these pests, but covering plants with insect-proof mesh can prevent egg-laying.

BULB DISEASES

Onion white rot is the most serious onion problem because it is virtually impossible to control and can persist in the soil for eight or more years. It also affects shallots, garlic and leeks. Initially, dense, white fungal growth develops on the base of the bulb, then small, black, resting bodies (that is, sclerotia) appear, and drop into the soil to affect subsequent crops. Leaves turn yellow as the roots rot. Dispose of affected plants as soon as symptoms of onion white rot are spotted. If no uncontaminated land is available, grow onions in containers of potting compost.

ONION, SHALLOT AND GARLIC PROBLEMS

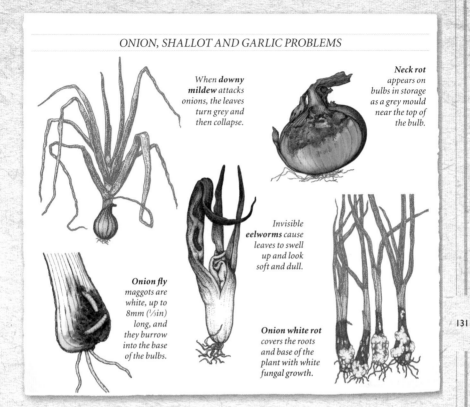

When **downy mildew** attacks onions, the leaves turn grey and then collapse.

Neck rot appears on bulbs in storage as a grey mould near the top of the bulb.

Invisible **eelworms** cause leaves to swell up and look soft and dull.

Onion fly maggots are white, up to 8mm (⅓in) long, and they burrow into the base of the bulbs.

Onion white rot covers the roots and base of the plant with white fungal growth.

STORAGE PROBLEMS

Onions should store well in a cool, dry place for many months, but can be affected by various problems. If kept too warm, they will tend to shoot and ultimately become unusable. A more serious problem is **neck rot**. The neck rotting fungus is picked up while the onion is still growing in the ground, but do not usually become a nuisance until the bulbs are stored. Affected bulbs start to turn soft, pale brown and semitransparent, then a dense, grey fungal growth develops and the bulb either rots or dries up. Other rots do not invade until the bulbs are in storage, producing blue-green moulds or causing the onions to turn slimy and smelly. The best way to prevent all these problems is to make sure onions are properly ripened with hard skins and firm flesh before storing in a clean, well-ventilated area. Check stores regularly and remove any rotten bulbs.

If canker can be avoided, parsnips are an easy crop to grow, if rather slow.

SEED PROBLEMS

Buy fresh parsnip seed each year as it does **not store well**. Parsnips can be very **slow to germinate** especially in cold weather so delay sowing until mid- or late spring outdoors.

ENVIRONMENTAL PROBLEMS

Contributory causes of **forked** root vegetables are likely to be stony or compacted soil, periods of drought, fresh manure in the soil or damage to roots when transplanting. If you find forked roots a real problem then choose a shorter-rooted variety, dig the soil to as fine a texture as you can manage to a depth of 30cm (1ft), incorporate bulky organic matter to retain moisture, and sow seeds direct in their final positions.

PEST PROBLEMS

Root aphids can develop as dense colonies on the shoulders of parsnip roots and the base of the leaves. They can reduce vigour but are difficult to control. Growing parsnips in different areas each year helps prevent numbers building up. **Celery leaf miner** can also

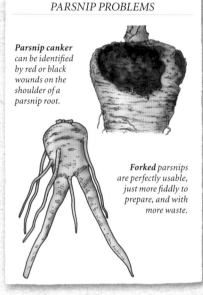

PARSNIP PROBLEMS

Parsnip canker *can be identified by red or black wounds on the shoulder of a parsnip root.*

Forked *parsnips are perfectly usable, just more fiddly to prepare, and with more waste.*

attack parsnip leaves, creating large pale patches that then turn brown (see p121). Parsnips are also susceptible to attacks from **carrot fly** (see p120).

DISEASE PROBLEMS

Parsnip canker can be caused by several different fungi, which greatly reduce a crop. Avoid it by planting resistant varieties in a fresh site each year and by avoiding any physical damage to the root tops through which fungi can enter. Canker thrives on acid soils, so add lime if the pH is below 6.5 (see p12).

132

• PEAS •

Peas, first grown in the Middle East, are one of the oldest plants in cultivation.

SEED AND SEEDLING PROBLEMS

Pea seeds are very attractive to **mice**. They are also prone to **rotting** in cold, wet soils. Avoid both these problems by starting peas off in pots. Home-saved pea seed may be attacked by **bean seed beetles** (see p110), and young pea plants by **pea and bean weevils** (see p111).

PEST PROBLEMS

Pea moth lays its eggs on pea flowers in summer. Treat plants with an insecticide approved for peas, or net plants with insect-proof mesh while in flower.

Pea thrips are tiny, narrow, sap-sucking insects that feed on leaves and pods, which turn silvery brown and may become distorted. Spray promptly with a suitable insecticide for use on peas.

DISEASE PROBLEMS

Powdery mildew can reduce yields. It is most prevalent in dry conditions, so try to ensure peas receive plenty of water and mulch along the rows to retain soil moisture. Also sow resistant varieties.

Pea viruses, spread by aphids, result in yellow or brown streaks and mottling on the foliage, followed by the plant collapsing. Dispose of affected plants.

Pea wilt affects peas and sweet peas (*Lathyrus odoratus*). Leaves rapidly turn yellow and plants collapse. Dispose of affected plants and grow peas on a different area of ground each year.

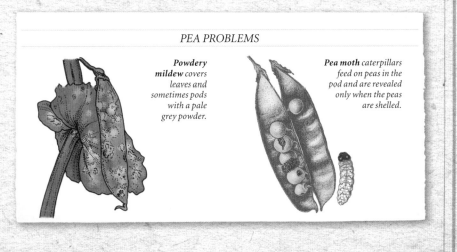

PEA PROBLEMS

Powdery mildew *covers leaves and sometimes pods with a pale grey powder.*

Pea moth *caterpillars feed on peas in the pod and are revealed only when the peas are shelled.*

• POTATOES •

Potatoes originate in the mountains of South America, but the species that evolved as the domestic potato is not frost hardy, so can be grown outdoors only during the warmer months. Potatoes are subject to attack by some devastating pests and diseases but with careful husbandry good crops are readily produced. Potatoes grow well in containers filled with potting compost or a mixture of soil and garden compost.

ENVIRONMENTAL PROBLEMS

Gardeners aim to plant potatoes as early as possible to get new potatoes by early summer. This makes them vulnerable to late **frosts**, which can blacken young foliage. More shoots generally grow, but such a set-back will delay cropping. Protect shoots against frost with fleece or plastic cloches – even a few layers of newspaper will help. Dig in plenty of bulky organic material where potatoes

POTATO BLIGHT

Late blight

Early blight

There are two kinds of potato blight. **Early blight** produces dark, angular spots on the foliage of potatoes and tomatoes, but it is not serious and rarely impacts on the crop. Unrelated **late blight** starts as large, yellow spots on the leaves. In warm, wet weather these spread rapidly, rotting the leaves and stems until the whole plant collapses. Affected tubers develop sunken patches with red/brown marks under the skin before being reduced to an evil-smelling pulp.

Early potatoes often avoid blight problems, and there are a few resistant maincrop varieties. Spraying with an appropriate fungicide approved for use on potatoes will help deter the disease. If it does strike, check all the tubers are covered with soil, then cut off all the foliage and dispose of it. This prevents fungal spores reaching the tubers which can be safely lifted two weeks later. Check stored potatoes regularly to remove any that start to rot. Late blight also affects tomatoes.

are to grow, to prevent lack of moisture and nutrients reducing crop yields.

LEAF PESTS

Colorado beetle is the most serious pest of potatoes in most areas, though it is absent from Britain and Ireland. The beetles and larvae feed on potato foliage, and can defoliate plants if numbers build up. Sightings in Britain must be reported to a police station or the Department for Environment, Food and Rural Affairs, so the beetles can be destroyed. Elsewhere, Colorado beetles can be excluded from the crop with insect-proof mesh, or be treated with an appropriate insecticide approved for potatoes, bearing in mind that the young larvae are much more vulnerable than other stages, and that Colorado beetles are resistant to many pesticides.

    Slugs (see p43) can also do significant damage to potato leaves and stems, and **aphids** (see p40) can be troublesome especially as they carry potato viruses

ROOT PESTS

Potato cyst eelworms attack plant roots, which function poorly, leading to yellowing of most of the lower foliage. Plants are often killed and few tubers produced. If you dig up affected plants

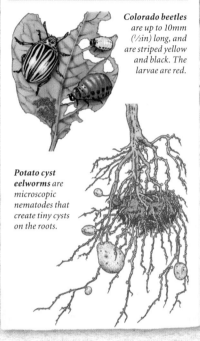

POTATO LEAF AND ROOT PROBLEMS

Colorado beetles *are up to 10mm (½in) long, and are striped yellow and black. The larvae are red.*

Potato cyst eelworms *are microscopic nematodes that create tiny cysts on the roots.*

135

you can see the pinhead-sized cysts, which may be white, golden yellow or brown, according to the species of eelworm involved. Nematode eggs in the cysts can remain viable in the soil for many years. Potato cyst eelworm also attacks tomato roots. There are no suitable pesticides available to gardeners for tackling this problem. Moving potatoes to different parts of the plot can help, though infestations may still build up. Some potato varieties

POTATO TUBER PROBLEMS

*Raised, dry, scabby patches on tubers are caused by **common scab**.*

*Arcs of brown discolouration – only seen when tubers are cut open – are known as **spraing**.*

__Black leg__ often appears on young plants, which develop yellow leaves then collapse as the stem rots. If plants survive, the tubers they produce are likely to rot.

*Small, soil-living **slugs** tunnel into potatoes, creating large cavities from small holes on the surface of the tuber.*

show resistance to one or more species of eelworm.

TUBER PESTS

When tubers are lifted, damage that has been caused underground may be revealed. **Slug** damage may be readily visible, though sometimes the slugs make only small holes on the surface then move into the tuber and eat it away from inside. These tubers can be used if the damage is cut away, but they will not store for long. The slugs are hard to control as they mostly live underground, though parasitic nematodes will reduce

their numbers (see p43). Lifting crops early can also help, because most slug damage is done in autumn. There are a number of less-susceptible potato varieties to try, too.

Millipedes and **woodlice** may be found inside potatoes hollowed out by slugs, but are not worth controlling.

Golden brown **wireworms**, about 2cm (¾in) long, also tunnel into potatoes. They mostly occur where grass has been dug over to make a vegetable patch and will decline in a few years. Lifting the crop as soon as the tubers are mature avoids the worst damage.

TUBER DISEASES

Common scab is the main problem noticed when tubers are lifted. It spoils the look of the potatoes, but has no effect on eating qualities. Scab is caused by a soil-dwelling bacterium, and is worst on light, sandy soils with little organic matter, and where the soil has been limed. Adding plenty of bulky organic matter will help minimise scab, and there are a number of resistant varieties.

Spraing is caused by viruses. These may also produce leaf symptoms such as yellow mosaics or splashes, but are often not serious and may go unnoticed. Viruses can build up if you save your own seed potatoes, so it is best to buy certified, virus-free stock at least every other year.

Black leg is caused by bacteria, and is nearly always brought into the garden on mildly infected tubers. The bacteria survive over winter principally in potato plant debris and infected volunteer tubers. Black leg attacks the stems near ground level, the foliage becomes yellow and stunted, the stems turn black and plants often die. If only some stems are affected, the plants may survive, but any tubers produced are likely to be

Carefully check potatoes for damage before putting them into storage.

infected and may rot in storage. Remove all affected plants, and dispose of their tubers. Choose resistant varieties and do not grow potatoes on the same ground for a few years.

STORAGE PROBLEMS

A variety of infections can damage stored potatoes, leading to **rotting**. Avoid this as far as possible by separating out any damaged potatoes and using them first. Store potatoes in a dry, cool but frost-free environment with some air flow, such as in wooden boxes or paper sacks, and check tubers regularly so that rotten ones can be removed.

137

• SPINACH •

Spinach has its origins in Iran and is closely related to beetroot and chard.

ENVIRONMENTAL PROBLEMS

Hot weather and dry soil encourage annual spinach's tendency to **bolt**, which then renders it useless as a crop. Avoid this by watering well and shading plants. If your spinach always seems to bolt, try chard (also known as perpetual spinach) which is a longer-lived plant.

SPINACH PROBLEMS

Spinach blight *starts with the younger leaves, turning them yellow and puckered, then spreads to the older ones.*

Spinach leaf spot *can be identified by pale grey or brown spots with a brown or purple halo.*

PEST PROBLEMS

Birds, such as pigeons, are rather partial to spinach, especially at times of year when there is little other greenery about. Protect plants with netting or, in cool periods, with horticultural fleece.

Slugs will also eat tender, green leaves. Hand picking on damp evenings, or drowning in slug traps, will reduce numbers. Copper rings are effective, but practical for only a small number of plants. Aluminium sulphate granules and ferric phosphate or metaldehyde pellets are also effective, but metaldehyde ones can be harmful to other creatures and children (see p43).

DISEASE PROBLEMS

Spinach blight is caused by cucumber mosaic virus (see p124). Destroy affected plants and control **aphids** (see p40).

Spinach leaf spot is not usually serious. Removing affected leaves helps control it. Spinach **downy mildew** causes yellow patches on the upper leaf surface, matched by grey-purple patches underneath. Removing outer leaves should help reduce humidity and may save the remainder. In future, choose resistant varieties and space plants so their leaves do not touch.

• SWEET CORN •

Sweet corn was developed from maize and is the only common vegetable that is a member of the grass family.

ENVIRONMENTAL PROBLEMS

Sweet corn is wind pollinated and so should be grown in a block, not in a long row, where the **pollen may blow away** from the other plants. Help pollination by tapping or shaking the plants.

PEST PROBLEMS

Seeds are often taken by **mice**, so set traps or sow seeds in a mouse-proof greenhouse. **Frit fly** lays its eggs on young sweet corn plants, and the small, white maggots can kill the shoots. Starting seeds off in pots in the greenhouse, or covering young plants with insect-proof mesh, should prevent attacks.

Ripening cobs can be targeted by **birds**, especially jays and pigeons, so net the whole crop, or cover the developing cobs with plastic or netting bags. **Badgers** love sweet corn, too – electric fencing should keep them out.

DISEASE PROBLEMS

Smut occurs only in long, hot summers. Control by removing any swellings before they burst and by growing sweet corn in a different spot each year.

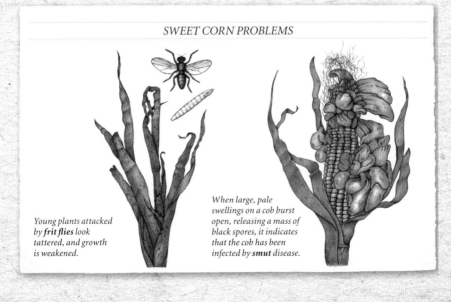

SWEET CORN PROBLEMS

Young plants attacked by **frit flies** look tattered, and growth is weakened.

When large, pale swellings on a cob burst open, releasing a mass of black spores, it indicates that the cob has been infected by **smut** disease.

• SWEET & CHILLI PEPPERS •

Gardeners in temperate regions generally grow peppers as annuals.

ENVIRONMENTAL PROBLEMS
Erratic watering can lead to **blossom end rot**. The immediate cause is lack of calcium, which is not being transported effectively. Although the fruit is still usable, the damage can encourage rotting. Provide a steadier water supply by raising plants individually in deeper containers; and avoid growing bags.

PEST-PROBLEMS
Peppers can suffer from **glasshouse whitefly** (see p44) and **glasshouse red spider mite** (see p42). **Greenfly** (see p40) tend to cluster under young leaves. Squash them or spray with a suitable insecticide.

Leaves and fruit can also be damaged by **tomato moth** caterpillars, which can be removed by hand. The adults are harder to spot as they tend to hide during the day. Shaking plants sometimes dislodges them. This moth also attacks glasshouse cucumbers and tomatoes.

DISEASE PROBLEMS
Grey mould (see p45) appears as a grey or brown, furry growth, usually on fruit or stems. It usually strikes when conditions are cold and damp. Good ventilation and removal of any dead leaves or immature fruit will help reduce attacks.

Cucumber mosaic virus (seee p.124) and **pepper mottle virus** can cause yellow patches and stunted foliage or fruit. Dispose of affected plants.

PEPPER PROBLEMS

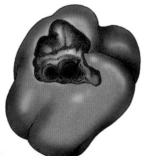

Blossom end rot can be identified by brown, sunken areas developing opposite the stalk, where the flower used to be.

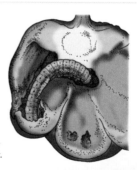

*Brown or green **tomato moth** caterpillars eat leaves and burrow into fruit.*

Like their close relation the potato, tomatoes seem prone to a wide range of problems but, with good cultivation, most of these can be overcome.

ENVIRONMENTAL PROBLEMS

Tomatoes grown under glass, or outdoors in containers, are often given high-potash feeds to encourage cropping. However, high-potash levels in the soil can inhibit the uptake of magnesium, so tomatoes can suffer from **magnesium deficiency** even when there is plenty in the soil. Therefore, do not overdose with such feeds and, if necessary, give additional magnesium in the form of Epsom salts (magnesium sulphate) as a foliar feed applied directly to the leaves in the evening.

Cold nights can cause tomato leaves to curl upwards. This does not damage the plants nor affect cropping.

Tomatoes are very susceptible to **damage by hormone weedkillers** – the type used to kill lawn weeds. Spray drift, or even storing weedkillers or equipment used to apply them, near tomatoes is enough to cause damage. Symptoms are usually quite distinctive and include distortion combined with very narrow, rolled-up leaves. Damage

is irreversible and, though plants sometimes grow out of it, they are likely to crop poorly.

Discoloured fruit can develop because of inappropriate growing conditions such as overheating or a shortage of nutrients. Both greenback and blotchy ripening include hard, green or yellow patches on the fruit, which does not then mature properly. Prevent these problems

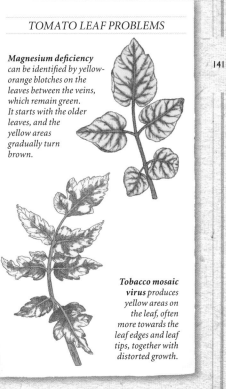

TOMATO LEAF PROBLEMS

Magnesium deficiency can be identified by yellow-orange blotches on the leaves between the veins, which remain green. It starts with the older leaves, and the yellow areas gradually turn brown.

Tobacco mosaic virus produces yellow areas on the leaf, often more towards the leaf edges and leaf tips, together with distorted growth.

141

TOMATO FRUIT PROBLEMS

Tomato blight *starts as yellow spots on foliage and also affects the fruits, which develop brown, dry-looking areas and do not ripen properly.*

Blossom end rot *appears as a brown, sunken area on the base of the tomato, with discoloured flesh underneath.*

Greenback *can be identified by a hard, green area that never ripens at the top of the fruit.*

Grey mould *may attack stems, fruit or leaves with its velvety, grey-brown fungal growth.*

by feeding the plants adequately and, under glass, by shading and ventilating their environment to keep temperatures down. Many modern tomato varieties are resistant to greenback.

Fruit **skin splitting** is the result of erratic watering. Avoid it by providing a steady water supply, adding organic matter to the soil and mulching outdoors, and shading or ventilating to prevent tomatoes grown under glass from getting too hot. Erratic watering also causes **blossom end rot** (see p140).

PEST PROBLEMS

Glasshouse whitefly is a serious pest in glasshouses, and badly affected plants become smothered in black, sooty mould growing on the honeydew excreted by the whitefly. Watch out for signs of their arrival and deal with them promptly (see p44). **Red spider mite** (see p42) can also attack tomatoes but is less problematic than on some glasshouse crops. **Tomato moth** can shred foliage and damage both ripe and developing fruit (see p140).

DISEASE PROBLEMS

The biggest problem with outdoor tomatoes, and sometimes with those grown under glass, is **tomato blight** – the same disease as late blight in potatoes (see p134). This usually affects leaves first, spreading rapidly in moist conditions to stems, which can blacken and collapse. Unripe fruit usually fails to develop, and ripe fruit can be unpalatable. Dispose of affected plants promptly. Prevent tomato blight by spraying with an appropriate fungicide suitable for use on tomatoes. A few varieties show some resistance.

Grey mould thrives in cool, moist conditions so is mostly a problem under glass in spring and autumn and outdoors in a wet season. It can affect stems, leaves and fruit; damaged ones should be pruned away promptly. Good hygiene and good ventilation are the best ways to minimise attacks.

A variety of **stem and root rots**, and **leaf moulds**, attack tomato plants, especially in cool, damp conditions. Young plants are often killed, and when fungi attack the base of the stem this can also kill older plants. Many of these fungi survive over winter on plant remains or in the soil or stored water, so clear up any debris at the end of the season, and do not grow tomatoes in the same area of soil year after year. Choosing resistant varieties, ensuring good ventilation, and careful watering with fresh water will help reduce these problems to a minimum.

A number of viruses attack tomatoes including **tobacco mosaic virus** (see p141), and these are easily spread to other plants on hands or tools – even on cigarettes. Tomato viruses produce a wide range of symptoms including yellow, bronze or dark green marks on foliage, dark streaks on stems and brown pits on fruit, stunted growth and distorted foliage. Remove and destroy all plants showing these symptoms because there is no treatment for viruses.

POOR FRUITING

Sometimes, tomato flowers drop without forming fruit, or small fruit appear but remain green and undeveloped (chats) or turn dry and brown (dry set). These problems are caused by a combination of dryness at the roots and poor pollination resulting from a dry atmosphere and cold nights. Keeping the soil moist, and tapping plant supports (to encourage the flowers to release pollen) or misting flowers with water every day, will help improve pollination.

FRUIT

• INTRODUCTION •

The problems you are likely to encounter when growing fruit in your garden or allotment include disorders arising from the plant's growing conditions as well as pests and diseases. Top fruit (fruit that grows on trees) is described first in this chapter, which covers apples, apricots, *cherries, peaches, pears, plums and quinces. This is followed by soft fruit (that is, fruit that grows on bushes and canes) and includes blackberries, black currants, blueberries, gooseberries, raspberries, red currants, strawberries and white currants – as well as grapes.*

• APPLES •

Apples can tolerate a surprising amount of damage from pests and diseases without it seriously impacting on the tree's overall health, and some problems can be largely ignored. However, other pests and diseases can have a significant effect on the quality and quantity of apples produced, so these need to be identified and controlled. Because apple trees may well grow and crop for 100 years, it is worth taking care to choose varieties that are suitable for your growing conditions. Some varieties are resistant to powdery mildew, scab, canker and some other problems, which greatly reduces the need for treatment.

ENVIRONMENTAL PROBLEMS

Bitter pit (see p151) occurs as a result of shortage of calcium in the fruit. This is not caused by a lack of calcium in the soil, but by problems with transporting it around the tree. Bitter pit is generally worse on dry soils, so watering in dry periods may help, as will mulching in spring with bulky organic material to improve water holding. Fruit with bitter pit can usually still be eaten, though it sometimes tastes bitter. Some apple varieties are particularly susceptible to bitter pit, and it is worth spraying these with calcium nitrate from early summer until early autumn.

LEAF PESTS

Various **moth caterpillars** feed on young apple leaves, flowers and developing fruit. They bind leaves together with silk, so often go unnoticed. The caterpillars are not worth worrying about unless

APPLE LEAF PROBLEMS

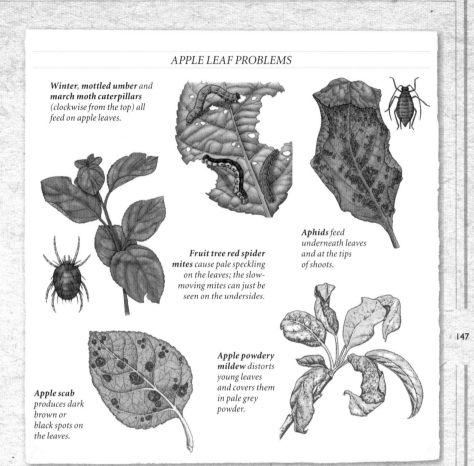

Winter, mottled umber and **march moth caterpillars** (*clockwise from the top*) *all feed on apple leaves.*

Aphids *feed underneath leaves and at the tips of shoots.*

Fruit tree red spider mites *cause pale speckling on the leaves; the slow-moving mites can just be seen on the undersides.*

Apple powdery mildew *distorts young leaves and covers them in pale grey powder.*

Apple scab *produces dark brown or black spots on the leaves.*

they appear in large numbers, in which case they can be picked off or sprayed before the flower buds open, using a suitable contact insecticide approved for apple The females of winter moth have rudimentary wings and cannot fly – they crawl up the trunks between midautumn and midspring, and can be trapped by grease bands, 15cm (6in) wide, fitted 1–1.5m (3–5ft) above the ground, or just below the lower branches on small trees.

Four species of aphid attack apple leaves. **Rosy apple aphids**, which are pink or grey and covered in a white wax powder, are the most damaging. They target shoots in early spring and their feeding activities can seriously distort young fruit, which then fails to develop. Squash colonies or, before the flower buds open, spray with a suitable insecticide approved for apple. **Rosy leaf-curling aphids** are blue-grey and turn the distorted leaves red; **apple grass aphids** are green and feed on leaf undersides; and **green apple aphids** are bright green or yellow green and attack new shoots. Although these three aphids are less damaging, you should squash large colonies, pick off the leaves or spray before or after flowering. These aphids overwinter as shiny, black eggs which can often be spotted on branches, and can be scrubbed off.

Fruit tree red spider mites cause pale speckling and bronzing on the leaves and their sap-sucking activities can weaken trees if numbers build up

in hot summers. There is no effective treatment for them.

LEAF DISEASES
Apple powdery mildew kills many young leaves, can have a stunting effect on young trees and reduces crops by attacking flower buds. The disease cannot be cured once established, so cut off and dispose of badly affected shoots. In future, use a suitable fungicide approved for use on fruit as a preventative treatment.

Scab does not cause that much damage to apple leaves, though they may drop prematurely. However, scab damage to fruit is more serious, and this disease is very disfiguring on crab apples. As soon as any spots are seen, spray with a suitable fungicide approved for use on fruit, and repeat at regular intervals through the season. Dispose of all infected leaves and cut out any cracked and scabby shoots to reduce carry-over of the scab spores to the next year.

Choosing disease-resistant varieties helps you to produce healthy fruit.

Woolly aphid forms fluffy, white patches on trunks and branches.

Crown gall affects the roots or the base of the trunk, producing a cluster of woody swellings, which can be as big as a football.

Apple canker produces dry, sunken pits, often with a rough and swollen edge, on twigs and branches.

TRUNK AND BRANCH PESTS

Woolly aphid is often mistaken for a fungus, because these insects cover themselves in white, waxy threads, forming fluffy, white patches on branches. They feed by sucking sap and usually do little damage in themselves, but the wounds they make in the bark can allow canker spores to enter. Scrub off colonies of woolly aphids with soapy water in spring, or treat with a systemic insecticide suitable for apple.

TRUNK AND BRANCH DISEASES

Apple canker is caused by a fungus that infects shoots, killing off areas of bark and the tissue beneath the affected patch. Cankered shoots break easily, new growth beyond the canker is weakened, and if cankers join up around a shoot or branch it will be killed. Control apple canker on small trees by spraying with an appropriate fungicide after harvest, and again when half the leaves have fallen. In addition, cut out twigs infected with canker in winter and pare back large cankers into healthy bark, then treat with wound paint. Resistant varieties are especially useful in areas with a wet climate.

Crown gall is caused by a bacterium. Although this disease appears dramatic, it rarely has any effect on plant growth. There is no treatment for crown gall, but improving drainage on wet soils should discourage it.

149

POOR FRUITING

If an otherwise healthy apple tree does not flower, it may be too young or or may have been overpruned so it is responding by growing vigorously and not fruiting. Time should sort out these problems. Apple trees grown from pips may not fruit for many years, and the fruit may be poor quality, so these are best replaced.

If the tree produces only a few flowers it may be prone to biennial bearing, ie, cropping every other year. Overcome this by removing about half the fruitlets produced in a good year as soon as they develop. It's also possible that birds have removed many of the flower buds. Netting small trees, or a few branches of large trees, is the only effective solution.

If there are plenty of flowers but few fruit, then late frosts may be the problem. These can kill the flowers and developing fruitlets, and also discourage pollinating insects or inhibit the pollination process itself. Pollinators are also deterred by windy weather.

Almost all apple varieties require another variety that flowers at the same time to allow for cross-pollination, and in the case of a few varieties, three trees are needed for pollination. The trees do not need to be that close, as bees fly considerable distances, and crab apples can pollinate apple flowers equally well. If you are buying trees, any fruit catalogue will help you choose apple varieties that will cross-pollinate each other.

FLOWER PESTS

Apple blossom may be damaged by **apple blossom weevil,** which lays its eggs on the flower buds. The resultant maggots eat away at the inside of the buds, which fail to open and go brown. The damage normally has little or no effect on yield. **Apple sucker** feeds on sap from flower buds and young leaves, turning them brown. Treatment is not usually needed, but if attacks have been serious in the past spray as the leaves start to open but before the flowers show any colour, using a contact insecticide approved for apple.

FRUIT PESTS

Codling moth lays its eggs on developing apples in summer. The caterpillars then tunnel into the centre of the fruits to feed, working their way out again a couple of months later. Affected fruit tends to ripen and drop early, and can be recognised by the exit hole, which usually has one or more coloured rings round it. When cut open, the apple is partly eaten, and the cavity filled with droppings. Affected fruit can be used, but will rot if stored. Reduce egg-laying by catching males in pheromone traps (see p35) hung in the trees in late spring.

Capsid bugs are long-legged insects,

APPLE FRUIT PROBLEMS

Slightly sunken, brown spots on the surface and small, brown marks in the flesh are symptoms of **bitter pit**.

Brown, rough patches on the skin are the scars from **capsid bug** *damage to the fruit while it is developing.*

Tunnels inside the fruit, and an exit hole with coloured haloes, will have been made by **codling moth** *caterpillars.*

4mm (⅙in) long. They feed by piercing young fruit, which develops rough scars on the skin. The damage is superficial, and not worth taking action against.

Birds and **wasps** can attack ripe fruit (see p152).

FRUIT DISEASES

Apple scab affects fruit as well as foliage, which develops olive-green to black spots on the skin. One or two spots are not serious, but bad infections can distort the fruit, and crack the skin, allowing in fungal rots. In future, look out for scab spots on leaves and spray with a suitable fungicide approved for use on fruit. Apples can also be affected by **brown rot** (see p155).

APPLE REPLANT DISEASE

If you plant apples where they have grown previously they will often fail to thrive. This problem is thought to be due to a species of soil-dwelling fungus called pythium, though there may be some other factors involved. If you need to plant in the same area either change the soil completely to a depth of 80–100cm (32–39in), or choose a stone-fruit tree (apricot, cherry, peach or plum) as these will not be affected, rather than one with pips (apple, pear, quince).

Pears suffer from many of the same problems as apples (see p146), and have a few pests and diseases of their own.

ENVIRONMENTAL PROBLEMS

Pears flower earlier than apples so are more likely to be caught by **frost**. Protect small trees with a double layer of fleece when frosts are forecast, or choose late-flowering varieties. Fruitlets can also be damaged, causing **russetting** – slightly rough, brown patches on the skin – which may inhibit proper development.

PEST PROBLEMS

Pear midge lays its eggs on unopened flower buds and the maggots later burrow into the fruitlets, eventually leaving to pupate in the soil. Break the life cycle by laying a cloth beneath the tree after flowering; collect and destroy all the affected fruitlets. Spray with a suitable insecticide when the blossom is at the white bud stage.

Pear sucker can attack blossom, and **codling moth** (see p150) may occasionally attack pear fruits. **Birds** and **wasps** are attracted to ripening fruit. Protect small trees with netting.

Large, pinky brown **pear bedstraw aphid** can infest young shoots in spring and cause serious distortion. If necessary, spray after flowering.

Pear leaf blister mite lives in small, raised lumps on the leaves. These lumps are often clustered together near the main vein, but seem to do no damage to a tree's overall health. Pick off small outbreaks. There is no practical way to control mites that have colonised the whole tree.

DISEASE PROBLEMS

Pear rust, which also affects several *Juniperus* species, produces spots on upper leaf surfaces and spiky, orange outgrowths on the undersides, which contain the spores. Limit small

QUINCES

The main problems with quinces are powdery mildew, which tends to attack young leaves, and quince blight, which affects older leaves and causes spotting on fruit and twig die-back. To control quince blight, collect up fallen leaves and fruit and prune out dead twigs; burn or bin everything. Spraying with a suitable fungicide as leaves open may give some control, as well as keeping powdery mildew in check.

PEAR AND QUINCE PROBLEMS

Fruitlets affected by **pear midge** blacken and fall early.

Pear leaf blister mite produces raised galls on leaves, which start off pale green, turn red and then black as the season progresses.

Fireblight normally attacks via pear flowers, and produces cankers at the base of infected shoots.

Irregular, large and small spots on leaves are caused by **quince blight**.

Vivid red or orange spots, often with a darker halo, are caused by **pear rust**.

outbreaks by destroying affected leaves. Apply a fungicide suitable for pears.

Shoots that blacken from the tip have probably been killed by **canker** (see p149) or **blossom wilt** (see p157). However, the cause may be **fireblight**, which is potentially fatal. Check the diagnosis by scraping the bark away from cankered areas and looking for red-brown staining. Cut back diseased stems to 50cm (20in) below the damage.

Stony pit produces fruit that is distorted by sunken areas on the surface, and has patches of hard, dead cells within the flesh. There is no cure. Replace badly affected trees. Pears can also suffer from **scab** (see p148) and **brown rot** (see p155).

Plums are prone to serious diseases, and late frosts can damage flowers and fruitlets, but if they escape these then overcropping may be the worst problem you face.

PEST PROBLEMS

Plum leaf-curling aphid seriously distorts the growth of new leaves, which become tightly curled and may die. Spray small trees as the leaves open, using a suitable insecticide approved for plums. Although disfiguring, mature trees seem to shrug off such attacks.

Plum leaf gall mite creates small, pale green bumps on plum leaves, especially round the edges. There is no effective control, but luckily the mites seem to have no effect on the health of a tree.

Plum fruit moth lays its eggs on developing fruit. The caterpillars tunnel into the fruits, which ripen and drop early. Collect affected fruit before the caterpillars leave to pupate. Male moths can be caught in pheromone traps (see p35). Alternatively, spray small trees in early summer and again three weeks later.

Plums are often targeted by **wasps**. Net small trees, or selected branches, with fine mesh to control them. Collecting up fallen fruit and hanging wasp traps in trees may reduce numbers.

DISEASE PROBLEMS

Silver leaf can attack any kind of fruit but is a particular problem with plums. It invades through wounds such as pruning cuts. The leaf silvering usually starts on one or two branches, then spreads through the tree. Branches more than 3cm (1in) in diameter develop a brown or purple stain on the internal tissues, which can be seen if a cut end is moistened. Small, bracket-shaped fruiting bodies may develop on older branches, purple at first, then brown or white. After the silvering appears, the branch usually dies back. Prune out affected branches to 15cm (6in) beyond the appearance of staining. There is no treatment for the disease but, as the spores are released in winter, pruning plum trees only in summer does reduce the risk of infection. There is also a condition known as **false silver leaf**, usually caused by poor growing conditions. This does not produce any other silver leaf symptoms such as dieback and staining, and can be overcome by feeding, watering and mulching.

Shothole is normally caused by a fungus that attacks cherry, peach and plum trees that are not growing well. Feed, water and mulch the tree, to

154

improve its vigour. Shothole can also be a symptom of the much more serious disease **bacterial canker** (see p157).

Plum rust starts as yellow spots on the leaf undersides, which then turn brown. The disease is not serious, and the main treatment is to feed, water and mulch to improve the tree's general health.

If large numbers of flowers turn brown but do not fall they have probably been affected by **blossom wilt** (see p157).

Plums that have been damaged by birds, insects, weather, or just knocking against each other can be affected by **brown rot**. There is no effective way to prevent it, though collecting up damaged fruit should reduce the number of spores. There are also some resistant varieties.

Pocket plum is caused by a fungus and produces fruit that is pale green, elongated and distorted, with no stone. Such fruit appears well before unaffected fruit develops. Where feasible, collect it up and destroy it, to reduce infection the following season. Spray small trees about three weeks before flowering with a fungicide approved for use on fruit.

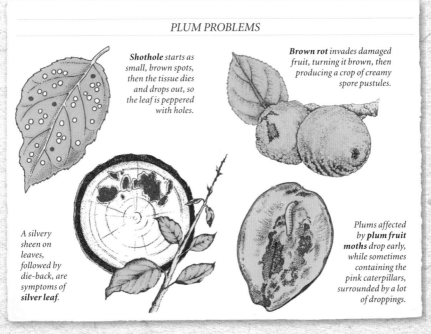

PLUM PROBLEMS

Shothole starts as small, brown spots, then the tissue dies and drops out, so the leaf is peppered with holes.

Brown rot invades damaged fruit, turning it brown, then producing a crop of creamy spore pustules.

A silvery sheen on leaves, followed by die-back, are symptoms of **silver leaf**.

Plums affected by **plum fruit moths** drop early, while sometimes containing the pink caterpillars, surrounded by a lot of droppings.

• APRICOTS, CHERRIES & PEACHES •

When successful, apricots, cherries and peaches are so delicious that the effort in growing them is worthwhile.

ENVIRONMENTAL PROBLEMS

Apricots and peaches flower in early spring, so the blossom and fruitlets can be destroyed by **frost**, and low temperatures discourage pollinating insects, both leading to crop failure. Cover trees in flower with two or three layers of fleece when frost is forecast; remove it on warmer days. If no pollinating insects are seen, transfer pollen from flower to flower using a soft paintbrush on a dry, warm day.

Peaches can suffer from **split stone**, which cracks the fruit at the stalk end, prevents proper ripening and lets in **brown rot** (see p155). The most common cause is an erratic water supply. Improve this by watering in dry periods and mulching the soil.

PEST PROBLEMS

Black peach aphids and yellow-green **peach-potato aphids** feed on peach trees in spring and early summer, causing leaves to yellow and crinkle.

Cherry blackfly cluster in dense colonies at shoot tips, causing severe

156

APRICOT, CHERRY AND PEACH PROBLEMS

One symptom of **bacterial canker** is the production of large amounts of gum from the trunk or branches.

Peach leaf curl develops as the foliage opens in spring, and creates large blisters that start red then produce a pale, powdery spore layer.

Blossom wilt causes all the flowers on an affected branch to turn brown and die, but they do not fall.

curling of the leaves, some of which will die off. Check new shoots early in the season and squash the insects or spray with an insecticide approved for use on these fruits – spray peaches after and cherries before flowering. With bad attacks, pick off affected leaf clusters.

Peaches are quite prone to attack by **brown scale insects** on leaves and branches (see p161).

DISEASE PROBLEMS

Bacterial canker is a problem on fruiting and ornamental cherries, apricots, peaches and plums. In spring, the buds on affected branches may fail to open at all or may start to develop but wither as the branch dies back. Bacterial canker can also produce brown spots on leaves; the tissue then dies and drops out, producing a similar effect to **shothole** (see p155). Cut out badly cankered branches in summer and treat the cuts immediately with wound paint. Spraying small trees with an appropriate fungicide in late summer and early and midautumn also helps to control the disease. There are some resistant varieties of cherry and plum.

Peach leaf curl affects peaches and nectarines, and rarely apricots. Leaves may become infected before or as they

PROTECTING WALL-GROWN FRUIT

Where an apricot, peach or cherry tree is grown against a wall or fence, it is well worth constructing a shelter to protect it. This can be covered with two or three layers of fleece in spring to protect the blossom from cold, and with netting in summer to keep off birds and wasps. If covered with polythene between midwinter and late spring, the tree will also be protected from peach leaf curl. The spores overwinter on the bark, but need rain to wash them into the opening buds to infect the leaves. Without rain, the spores do not develop.

157

develop, in spring. Remove all affected leaves before the bloom of fungal spores appears. Spray with an appropriate fungicide when the leaves fall in autumn and twice more, two weeks apart, in mid- or late winter. Otherwise, protect the tree against this disease (see box above).

Cherries seem particularly prone to **blossom wilt**. It is worst in wet springs. Where possible, prune out and dispose of affected shoots in summer. The following year, spray with an appropriate fungicide just before the flowers open and repeat a week later.

Apricots, cherries and peaches are also susceptible to **silver leaf** (see p154).

• BLUEBERRIES •

Blueberries succumb to few pests or diseases, but soil type is crucial.

ENVIRONMENTAL PROBLEMS

Plants must not be allowed to **dry out** and they require very acid soil, with a pH of 5.5 or less. If you live in a hard water area, collect rainwater to use on your blueberries. However, tap water is preferable to letting the plants dry out.

If grown in soil or compost with too high a pH, plants will develop **lime-induced chlorosis** (see p83), that is, they turn yellow. Treat with sequestered or chelated iron or move plants into soil with a lower pH.

PEST PROBLEMS

Squash **aphids** or spray with a suitable insecticide. Netting stretched taut over a frame gives good **bird** protection.

Yellowing between the veins is a sign that a plant lacks iron because there is too much lime in the soil.

158

BLUEBERRY PEST

*Fruit-eating **birds**, such as blackbirds and thrushes, can quickly strip blueberry bushes of their produce.*

FAILURE TO PRODUCE FLOWERS AND FRUIT

If your blueberries do not flower, you could be overfeeding them or pruning too much. They do not need pruning at all in the first two years and, after that, need only about a third of the oldest branches cutting down to the ground. Flowers forming but no fruit could be caused by cold weather damaging the flowers or discouraging flying insects. Try moving plants in flower to a sunnier, more sheltered position and protecting them with two layers of horticultural fleece on frosty nights. Although some blueberries are self-fertile, you will get much better crops if you grow two or three varieties, which can then cross-pollinate.

• CURRANTS •

Black, red and white currants are closely related, with red and white currants being variants of the same species. Black currants are probably the easiest to grow, but for all three good cultural conditions and correct pruning should ensure a worthwhile crop, even if problems occur. Use netting to protect ripening berries from birds.

ENVIRONMENTAL PROBLEMS

Some black currant varieties flower in early spring, and are vulnerable to **frost** damage, though other early-flowering varieties are more resistant. If bushes have been damaged in the past, then protect them in frosty periods with a double layer of horticultural fleece. If planting new currants, choose frost-tolerant or later-flowering varieties.

BUD PESTS

Before the buds on black currants even open, they can be attacked by **big bud mites** (see p160). These microscopic creatures feed

Black currants are highly productive, and the easiest currant to grow.

in the buds in large numbers. Usually only a small percentage of buds are affected, so the appearance of big bud in itself is not that significant. However, the mites also carry **reversion virus**, which seriously affects cropping (see box p161).

LEAF PESTS

Currant blister aphids (see p160) are the most dramatic pest of currants, though the overall damage to plant health is not serious. They produce red blisters on red and white currants and, less often, yellow blisters on black currants. Other aphids can distort developing shoots. Once the damage is seen, it is too late to take action, so if aphids are a regular problem spray with an insecticide suitable for use on currants, as soon as the buds open.

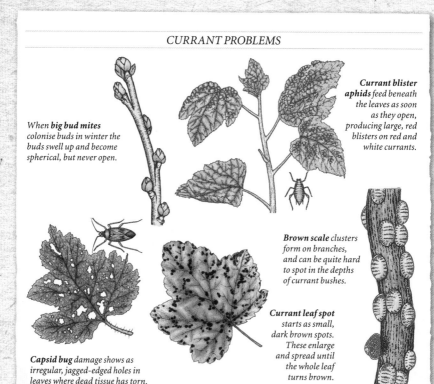

CURRANT PROBLEMS

When **big bud mites** colonise buds in winter the buds swell up and become spherical, but never open.

Currant blister aphids feed beneath the leaves as soon as they open, producing large, red blisters on red and white currants.

Brown scale clusters form on branches, and can be quite hard to spot in the depths of currant bushes.

Currant leaf spot starts as small, dark brown spots. These enlarge and spread until the whole leaf turns brown.

Capsid bug damage shows as irregular, jagged-edged holes in leaves where dead tissue has torn.

Capsid bugs can attack all types of currant, producing distinctive, ragged holes in the leaves. Control is difficult because the pests are very mobile, but spraying as the leaves open, using an insecticide approved for currants, may reduce damage. Also, spray the ground under the bush to catch capsids that have dropped to the ground.

Gooseberry and other **sawfly** larvae sometimes attack currants (see p162).

LEAF DISEASES

Currant leaf spot, which affects currants and gooseberries, can appear from late spring. Affected leaves fall early, causing the bushes to lose vigour. Disease spores overwinter on the leaves, so collect these up and dispose of them. There are no chemical controls.

Black currants can be affected by **American gooseberry mildew** (see p162). This covers leaves and fruit in white powder and can distort the growth of shoots. The symptoms are less severe than on gooseberries, but affected shoots should be cut out and disposed of. Preventative spraying with an appropriate fungicide can reduce attacks, and there are some resistant varieties.

STEM PESTS

Currant clearwing moth caterpillars tunnel into young stems, usually of black currants, in summer. They go unnoticed until the hollowed-out stems snap. Look out for affected shoots in winter and prune them out.

Brown scale can attack all types of currant. Their sap-sucking activities can weaken plants. Small numbers can be rubbed off, otherwise use an insecticide approved for currants.

STEM DISEASES

Coral spot can be a serious problem on red currants. This fungus usually starts on dead shoots, producing salmon-pink spore clusters, but can spread to live shoots and ultimately kill the plant. Remove and burn any affected shoots as soon as possible, cutting well back into sound, healthy wood and treating the cut shoots with wound paint immediately. Clear away any dead wood or old timber in the vicinity, because this can harbour the disease.

REVERSION VIRUS

This is the most serious disease of black currants and is caused by a virus-like organism that is spread by big bud mites. It does not affect other currants. The symptoms of reversion are subtle: new shoots develop abnormal leaves that are somewhat narrower, with fewer veins, than healthy ones, though the colour is unaffected; and the flower buds lose the downy covering, which usually gives them a grey appearance, to reveal the magenta colour underneath. Destroy affected bushes as there is no control for this disease. Replant with virus-free stock in a different area.

• GOOSEBERRIES •

Gooseberries go on cropping regardless, but you may need to net against birds.

ENVIRONMENTAL PROBLEMS

Gooseberry flowers can be damaged by late **frosts**, so protect them with a double layer of fleece when appropriate.

Fruit left to ripen may **split**, then rot, unless plants are watered in dry periods and mulched. Pick fruit before it rots.

PEST PROBLEMS

Gooseberry sawfly larvae feed voraciously in groups. Check plants regularly, especially in the centre of the bush, and hand pick or spray with an insecticide approved for gooseberry. The loss of leaves will weaken the plant.

Plants may be attacked by aphids, including **gooseberry aphids**, and by **capsid bugs** (see p160).

DISEASE PROBLEMS

American gooseberry mildew distorts shoots and damages fruit. Discourage it by keeping plants watered and mulched, and by pruning to improve air movement. Cut out and dispose of affected shoots in early autumn. As the flowers start to open, spray with a suitable fungicide approved for use on fruit. There are several resistant varieties.

Grey mould can cause die-back, and may kill the whole plant. Cut out and burn affected shoots. Plants can also be affected by **currant leaf spot** (see p160).

162

GOOSEBERRY PROBLEMS

*The caterpillar-like larvae of **gooseberry sawfly** can completely defoliate bushes if left unchecked.*

American gooseberry mildew starts on leaves and shoots as a white, powdery covering. On fruit, it becomes pale brown and felt-like.

• GRAPES •

Grapevines are able to shrug off most problems, especially if grown outdoors.

ENVIRONMENTAL PROBLEMS
Magnesium deficiency generally shows as yellow-orange or purple blotches between the veins. Spray with Epsom salts (magnesium sulphate) at once and then in two and four weeks.

PEST PROBLEMS
Stems can become infested by scale insects including **brown scale** (red-brown, shiny insects, 6mm/¼in long) and **woolly vine scale** (brown, wrinkled insects, 6mm/¼in long, with a white egg sac). **Mealybugs** (see p67) are pinkish brown, covered in white, waxy scales, and tend to cluster in joints between stems. Scrape off loose bark in winter and spray these with insecticide in midsummer.

Sap-sucking **red spider mites** (see p42) can do significant damage.

Both **birds** and **wasps** can be serious pests of grapes grown outdoors, so grow grapes inside a fruit cage, or enclose individual bunches in net bags.

DISEASE PROBLEMS
Powdery mildew thrives in crowded conditions especially where plants are

GRAPE PROBLEMS

Powdery mildew can be identified by a white, powdery coating on leaves, young shoots and developing fruits.

Grey mould usually enters via the dying flowers but does not appear until the fruit is nearly ripe, covering it with fuzzy fungal growth beneath which the fruit rots.

dry at the roots. Affected berries tend to split and cease growing. Prevention is the best approach, so thin growth out and keep plants well ventilated. Water in dry spells and mulch to retain moisture. If necessary, spray with a suitable fungicide approved for use on fruit.

Grey mould thrives in cool, damp conditions. Remove affected bunches. In future, thinning bunches may help.

Raspberries can be susceptible to a range of disease problems that tend to build up over time. Rather than worrying too much about trying to deal with all of these potential problems every year, the simple approach is just to replace all the canes every 8–10 years, ideally planting them on a different area of ground.

ENVIRONMENTAL PROBLEMS

Raspberries are quite fussy about their growing conditions. They prefer to be located in a slightly acid soil, ideally pH6–6.5 (see p12), with a high organic content so it is easy for their fine roots to penetrate and extract the moisture needed for good growth.

In alkaline soils, raspberries may suffer from **iron deficiency**, which tends to affect younger leaves first, starting as a yellowing between the veins but sometimes turning leaves completely yellow. It is not practical to make garden soils more acidic, so if you have a **limy soil** either grow raspberries in tubs or treat them annually with a product

164

RASPBERRY LEAF AND FRUIT PROBLEMS

Lime-induced chlorosis starts as a yellowing between the veins, and can turn the whole leaf yellow.

Irregular, yellow patches, sometimes with distorted growth, indicate the presence of **raspberry mosaic virus**.

Small, brown **raspberry beetles** *lay their eggs on the flowers, and the resultant grubs feed on the berries, leading to dry, grey patches especially at the stalk end.*

Leaf and bud mites *also cause yellow spotting on leaves, but no other damage.*

containing sequestered or chelated iron. Raspberries are also prone to **magnesium deficiency**, especially in wet springs. This tends to affect older leaves, where it appears as yellow-orange patches between the veins. Treat by applying a foliar feed of Epsom salts (magnesium sulphate).

LEAF AND FRUIT PESTS

Raspberry beetle larvae damage fruit, but it can still be eaten. Usually the larvae themselves have left by the time the fruit is picked. Control this pest by catching the adults with a pheromone trap (see p35) or, when the first pink fruit develops, by spraying with a suitable insecticide approved for raspberry. Autumn-fruiting varieties suffer less damage by raspberry beetle.

Several species of **aphids** (see p40) infest the leaves, shoot tips and flowers of raspberries during summer. As well as the direct damage of their sap-sucking activities, aphids also spread several viruses. Control them by spraying in midspring with an insecticide approved for use on raspberry. Some varieties are resistant to aphid attack.

Leaf and bud mite is a microscopic pest that lives on the undersides of the leaves, resulting in yellow blotches.

BLACKBERRIES

Blackberries can suffer from many of the same pests and diseases as raspberries, but are generally affected less often and less seriously. They can be also attacked by red berry mites, which live unnoticed on the leaves during summer; these pests then move onto the developing berries, inhibiting ripening so part or all of the berry remains red. Such fruit can still be cooked, but will never ripen properly.

These can look similar to virus symptoms, but the mites' activities have no other effect on the plant, so they can safely be ignored.

Birds, **squirrels** and **other mammals** will take raspberries if they get the opportunity. The only effective way to prevent this is to exclude them with netting. Keep this taut by stretching it over a frame to prevent wildlife becoming entangled.

LEAF DISEASES

Raspberry rust appears first on the upper surface of the leaf as small, orange, powdery spots. Later in the season, dark brown spots develop on the undersurface and the leaves fall prematurely. Rust does not seem to

*Canes affected by **grey mould** become silvery or pale in colour and die back. Grey, velvety areas may appear in wet weather.*

***Cane spot** can be identified in early summer by small, purple spots that grow up to 6mm (¼in) across then develop into cankers.*

***Cane blight** attacks at ground level, turning the base of the cane black and brittle. Leaves on affected canes wither in summer.*

***Spur blight** appears as dark purple blotches in late summer; these turn silver with minute, black spots. Neighbouring buds either die or produce short-lived shoots.*

166

affect the plants seriously, but it is worth collecting up and disposing of affected leaves. Some older varieties are particularly prone to this disease.

Raspberries are susceptible to half-a-dozen viruses collectively known as **raspberry mosaic virus** (see p164) as they produce similar, yellow blotches on the leaves. There may be some distortion too, and over time yield will be severely reduced. At this point, you should replace the plants. Some viruses can be avoided by controlling aphids and by choosing resistant varieties, while others are spread by eelworms or even pollen and these cannot be prevented.

CANE PESTS

Brown scale (see p160) can infest raspberry canes and should be scraped off when spotted.

CANE DISEASES

Raspberries can suffer from four specific fungal diseases: **grey mould**, **cane spot**, **cane blight** and **spur blight**. All result in canes either dying or producing stunted growth. Cut out affected canes as low down as possible and burn or bin. Spraying with a fungicide suitable for raspberries in spring and again in early summer should help prevent outbreaks. There are some resistant varieties.

Strawberries appear to be prone to more than their fair share of pests and diseases, some of which can be pretty devastating, but perseverance is worthwhile for the delicious end-product.

ENVIRONMENTAL PROBLEMS

Flowers that develop **black eye** will die without producing any fruit. Prevent this happening by protecting plants from frost when in flower, using cloches or a double layer of horticultural fleece. Remove this in warm spells to allow access to pollinating insects. Lack of pollination, often caused by cold or windy weather discouraging pollinators, leads to **distorted fruit**.

Strawberries can be soiled and **damaged** when in contact with the soil, so protect them with straw, strawberry mats or black plastic laid around the plants when they start to flower.

LEAF AND ROOT PESTS

Strawberry plants are so susceptible to **vine weevils** that they are used as an indicator plant to test how badly infested a piece of ground may be. The vine weevil grubs tunnel into the crown of the plant, and feed on the roots. Frequently, the first sign of trouble is when the plant collapses and can just be lifted free of the ground. The white, C-shaped grubs may be spotted in

167

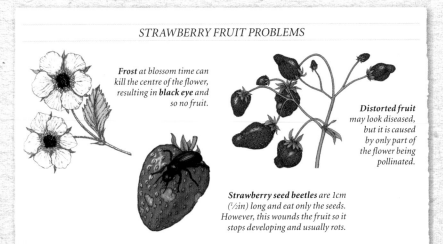

STRAWBERRY FRUIT PROBLEMS

*Frost at blossom time can kill the centre of the flower, resulting in **black eye** and so no fruit.*

Distorted fruit may look diseased, but it is caused by only part of the flower being pollinated.

Strawberry seed beetles are 1cm (½in) long and eat only the seeds. However, this wounds the fruit so it stops developing and usually rots.

the remains of the crown. For control methods see p44.

Aphids (see p40) feed by sucking sap from the leaves and can check growth if present in large numbers, as well as spreading viral disease. Control them before the flowers open, using an insecticide approved for strawberry. Do not spray plants while in flower as this can damage harmless insects.

Red spider mites (see p42) also feed on leaves and can cause considerable damage in hot, dry summers. Look out for pale mottling on the leaves and spray with an insecticide approved for use on strawberry, before the leaves start to turn yellow and dry out.

Choose virus-free plants to get your strawberries off to a good start.

LEAF AND ROOT DISEASES

Most strawberries are susceptible to **powdery mildew** (see p47), especially towards the end of the season. It turns the leaves purple on top and powdery grey underneath, and may kill some of the foliage. **Strawberry leaf spot** is usually less serious than powdery mildew. If fruiting has finished, treat both these problems by cutting off all the leaves and stalks back to the crown; then clear away straw and any other debris, and burn or bin it. There are no chemical controls for these diseases.

Strawberries can be affected by a number of **viruses** that appear as yellow or purple blotches on the leaves together with significant stunting and loss of crop. Dig up and dispose of affected plants. Check that any new plants are certified virus free.

If plants wither and collapse, but the roots are still intact, the likely cause is one of several root diseases, including **verticillium wilt** (see p49), **black root rot** and **red core disease**. These diseases are soilborne, tend to be worse in wet soils and cannot be treated. Dig up and dispose of affected plants, and plant any replacements in a different site.

FRUIT PESTS

The main pests are **birds** and **slugs**. Keep birds off with netting stretched over hoops until it is taut, to avoid trapping the birds. Use 1.5cm (½in) mesh so that pollinating insects are not excluded. For slug control see p43. **Strawberry seed beetles** (see p167) feed mostly on weed seeds, so keeping weeds under control should help to deter them.

FRUIT DISEASES

Grey mould (see p45) can affect all soft fruit but is a particular problem with strawberries, especially in wet weather.

STRAWBERRY LEAF AND ROOT PROBLEMS

Red core disease produces a red-brown discolouration in the centre of the roots.

Strawberry leaf spot starts as small, red-purple spots that expand and develop a silvery centre.

169

Rain can physically damage the soft-skinned fruit and damp conditions encourage the fungus. Berries develop a grey, furry coating and rapidly rot, and the disease can spread to other parts of the plant. Prompt removal of all affected parts should reduce the problem. If crops are repeatedly damaged, it can be worth protecting them with cloches or low polytunnels, though these need to be open-ended and not too long, to allow access to pollinating insects.

WEEDS

• INTRODUCTION •

Weeding is a necessary chore, but the more you can do to prevent weeds growing in the first place the less weeding you have to do. It therefore helps to understand the *characteristics of annual and perennial weeds and how to deal with them as well as how to identify and control a range of common weeds.*

• PREVENTING WEEDS •

Weeds spoil the look of an attractive border or well-kept lawn. More importantly, they compete for space, moisture and nutrients with the plants you want to grow, and may harbour pests and diseases. Most weeds increase by seed, even if they can also spread underground roots.

Your first line of defence, therefore, is never to allow weeds to set seed, even if this means just pulling off the flowers and dealing with the rest of the plant later. You should also never put weeds with flowers or seedheads into the compost bin. Domestic compost heaps rarely get hot enough to kill weed seeds, so this material is better consigned to large-scale community or municipal schemes, or you can dry and burn them.

Areas that are not cultivated, such as paths and drives, can treated with long-term, residual weedkillers (see p177), which remain in the soil and prevent new weeds developing. Areas of weed-free ground can be kept that way by using mulches. These are laid over the surface of the soil, and come in a number of guises: loose, organic; loose, non-organic; and sheet mulches.

LOOSE, ORGANIC MULCHES

Such mulches are only effective in suppressing weeds growing from seed, and must be at least 5cm (2in) deep. They will not deter shoots growing up from underground stems, bulbs, tubers or roots of weeds that are already established, so these must be thoroughly cleared from the ground before the mulch is put down.

Loose, organic mulches include garden compost, well-rotted farmyard manure and mushroom compost. In addition to smothering any weed seedlings, they also help to retain moisture in the soil and provide some nutrients.

Uncomposted grass clippings are very effective at retaining moisture in the soil, and at suppressing weeds, so can be used to good effect in the vegetable or fruit plot, or among shrubs, where appearance is not important. Chipped bark looks attractive but is too open-textured to be very effective as a weed suppressant or for moisture retention.

LOOSE, NON-ORGANIC MULCHES

Gravel and pebbles can be effective both to suppress weed seedlings and to retain moisture in the soil. Over time, they tend to sink into the soil so either top them up regularly or lay them over a water-permeable sheet mulch.

SHEET MULCHES

These include temporary coverings such as cardboard, old carpet and thin, black plastic as well as long-term materials such as woven polypropylene or compressed fibre sheets. Temporary coverings are useful to clear the ground of weeds by depriving them of the light needed for growth. Long-term materials are highly effective at preventing weed seeds from germinating. They can also be used to suppress very problematic weeds such as horsetail (see p180) that cannot be completely eradicated. Long-term sheet mulches should be permeable, and can be covered with a thin layer of bark or gravel to improve their appearance.

PLANTING THROUGH A SHEET MULCH

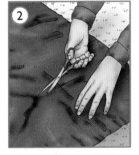

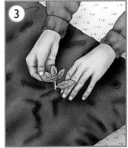

Anchor the sheet mulch by burying the edge, or weighing it down with bricks or timber.

Cut a cross where you want to plant and open out the flaps.

Plant as usual, water well and fold back the flaps.

• ANNUAL WEEDS •

Annuals flower and die in less than a year. This means that they do not have time to produce very extensive root systems, and have no need to develop underground storage to get them through winter. Common annual weeds are hairy bittercress (see p180), groundsel, shepherd's purse and annual meadow grass. They are quick to colonise any available space, and luckily they are relatively easy to control.

HOEING

A major reason why vegetables are grown in rows is so that it is easy to distinguish between wanted and unwanted plants when hoeing. This remains a quick and effective technique for dealing with small weeds if carried out with a sharp hoe on a dry day when the weeds will quickly shrivel. Make sure weeds are hoed off before they set seed.

HANDWEEDING

When conditions are too wet, the weeds are too big, or there is no room to manoeuvre a hoe, then hand pulling is required. Using a hand fork makes it easier to get all the roots out.

MULCHING

A thick layer of mulch (see p172) can kill small weed seedlings, and will generally prevent seeds germinating successfully.

CONTROLLING ANNUAL WEEDS

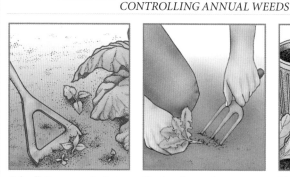

To be effective, you need a sharp hoe to sever the weeds just below ground level.

Handweeding may be necessary to remove larger weeds, where there is little space or in wet conditions.

Mulching weed-free, moist ground helps suppress annual weeds and retain soil moisture.

NON-NATIVE WEEDS

Most garden weeds are just native plants that are very successful colonisers of open ground, growing where you do not want them. However, there is increasing concern about a small group of overseas plants originally introduced into gardens as ornamentals and now causing problems not only in gardens but also in the countryside. Here, they can smother natural vegetation, block waterways, cross-breed with native species or deprive wildlife of its natural food or habitat. The most notorious of these plants is Japanese knotweed (*Fallopia japonica*), and it is an offence to allow this to escape into the wild. The same is true of giant hogweed (*Heracleum mantegazzianum*), and a number of other plants, including several troublesome aquatic weeds (eg Himalayan balsam/*Impatiens glandulifera*), are under consideration for the same legislation. For gardeners the advice is simple: don't plant these few, problematic plants in gardens and always compost, dry or burn excess garden plants – never dump them or allow them to spread by roots or seeds beyond the garden's boundaries.

Japanese knotweed is a long-lived perennial and can regrow from tiny pieces of deep-rooted rhizome, making digging impractical. Repeated spraying with a systemic weedkiller is needed for full control.

Giant hogweed plants live for only two or three years, but seeds can survive 15 years in the soil. Pull up seedlings, cut down larger plants, or use weedkiller but keep the sap off your skin because it can cause severe blistering.

Himalayan balsam is an annual, but spreads rapidly from seed, especially along watercourses. Control it by cutting plants down before they flower.

WEEDKILLERS FOR ANNUALS

It is rarely necessary to use weedkillers to deal with annual weeds in cultivated areas. Contact weedkillers (see p177) may be needed to kill weeds that are hard to pull up, such as in paving cracks, and residual weedkillers (see p177) are useful on paths and drives.

• PERENNIAL WEEDS •

Perennial weeds live for several years, and range in size from the daisies in your lawn to the bramble rampaging through your hedge. Most are herbaceous, dying down to the ground each winter. They have developed a range of strategies for survival including storage roots, tubers, bulbs and underground stems. These storage organs are one reason why perennial weeds are so difficult to eradicate. The taproots of thistles (see p179) and dandelions, the tubers of lesser celandine and oxalis (see p182) or the underground stems of couch grass (see p178) and horsetail (see p180) are all examples of these storage organs. A few perennial weeds, such as bramble and wild rose, do not have storage roots so, once dug out, they will not regrow.

DIGGING

Perennial weeds can be controlled by digging, especially on regularly cultivated ground such as a vegetable plot or border full of bedding plants. However, many perennials can regrow from root fragments so every bit must be removed, otherwise digging can actually make the situation worse.

MULCHING

Loose mulches, such as garden compost, bark or gravel (see p172), will have little effect on established perennials as they will just push through them. However, sheet mulches (see p173), when left in place for months, can be an effective way to clear ground of many perennials, and prevent them becoming re-established.

CONTROLLING PERENNIAL WEEDS

Remove all traces of perennial weeds to prevent them regrowing.

Use a dedicated watering-can and dribble bar to apply liquid weedkillers.

WEEDKILLERS FOR PERENNIALS

Careful use of weedkillers is often the most effective way of dealing with perennial weeds. To clear an area of ground, wait until the weeds are growing well, then treat with a systemic weedkiller. Retreatment may be needed with some particularly persistent weeds, so in areas that are going to be planted permanently always allow time for regrowth and retreatment. It is worth losing a growing season to be sure you are starting off with weed-free ground.

UNDERSTANDING WEEDKILLERS

There are four main groups of weedkillers. These act in different ways and are used for different situations.

● **Contact weedkillers** destroy the leaves and soft stems of weeds. This will kill many annuals, but most perennials will regrow.

● **Systemic weedkillers** are absorbed by the weed and carried in the sap above and below ground. This means they will kill both annual and perennial weeds.

● **Selective weedkillers** kill some kinds of plant and not others. For example, the hormone weedkillers used on lawns affect only broadleaved weeds, not narrow-leaved grasses.

● **Residual weedkillers** remain on the surface of the soil, preventing weed growth for several months. They can be used in plant-free areas such as paths or, with care, among woody plants.

USING WEEDKILLERS

Follow these tips to ensure you are handling weedkillers safely and effectively.

- Apply chemical weedkillers only when necessary. Other effective ways to deal with weeds are outlined in this chapter.
- Check the general safety guidelines for all chemicals.
- Know what weeds you have and choose an appropriate weedkiller.
- Unless you have large areas to clear, a ready-to-use weedkiller spray is often the most practical choice.
- If using a diluted concentrate, apply it with a watering-can and dribble bar, because this is easier to control than a sprayer and makes drift less likely. Do not use this can for any other job.
- Keep children and animals out of the treated area until the product is dry, or for as long as the manufacturer recommends, as stated on the label.

BROADLEAVED DOCK

Such docks (*Rumex obtusifolius*) tend to grow unnoticed at the backs of borders or the bottom of hedges, but if allowed to seed young plants can appear anywhere, root strongly and prove very resistant to being pulled out. In open ground, large dock plants can be dug out. However, the main roots are thick and branching, and you must remove the upper 15cm (6in) of these roots to prevent regrowth. This makes the process too disruptive in many areas of the garden. The alternative is to use a systemic weedkiller, taking care not to treat any wanted plants alongside. In lawns and paved areas, tackle individual rosettes of broadleaved dock with ready-to-use sprays or other appropriate spot treatments.

COUCH GRASS

The most troublesome grass weed in beds and borders is couch grass or twitch (*Elymus repens*), which spreads rapidly through its rhizomes (creeping underground stems). These can extend by 1m (3ft) or more each year, and dense patches can choke out delicate plants. The sharp tips of the rhizomes can pierce sheet mulches and pond liners. Couch grass does not root deeply so is relatively easy to dig out from open ground. Make sure all fragments of the tough rhizomes are removed or these will regrow. On uncultivated areas, spray with a systemic weedkiller. Among other plants, use a systemic weedkiller that is deactivated on soil contact, protecting any wanted plants from the spray.

178

BROADLEAVED DOCK

COUCH GRASS

CREEPING THISTLE

As its name implies, creeping thistle (*Cirsium arvense*) colonises new ground via its root system, which spreads extensively forming a network of interconnected growths so that a large patch of thistles may consist of a single plant. It can also spread by seed. Hoe off seedlings and small plants, but you will need to dig out older plants, taking care to remove all the roots as small fragments will regrow. Patches of thistles can be weakened by repeatedly cutting back just before the flower buds open. Otherwise, use a systemic weedkiller at the same stage, keeping nearby plants covered until the weedkiller is dry. Treat individual plants with ready-to-use sprays or other spot treatments before they produce flowering stems.

FIELD BINDWEED

There are two common types of bindweed: field bindweed (*Convolvulus arvensis*), which produces a cluster of stems radiating across the ground like a star and has small, pink flowers; and hedge bindweed or bellbine (*Calystegia sepium*), which has several vigorous shoot that usually twine round each other as they spread and bears large, white flowers. Hedge bindweed is much more vigorous, but only field bindweed regularly produces seeds. Both have fleshy, brittle, white rhizomes, which spread rapidly, break easily and can penetrate 2m (6½ft) into the ground. These make eradication by digging alone almost impossible, so treat with a systemic weedkiller in summer or autumn as well.

CREEPING THISTLE

FIELD BINDWEED

FIELD HORSETAIL

Also known as marestails, field horsetail (*Equisetum arvense*) belongs to a very ancient group of plants; their giant ancestors provided the raw material that produced coal. They develop no flowers or leaves but reproduce by means of powder-like spores. Their black, underground stems spread wide and deep and are hard to spot. Frequent hoeing or digging can help to keep field horsetail in check, but it is virtually impossible to eradicate in this way as shoots can regrow from deep below ground. Long-term smothering with sheet mulches stops it shooting but does not seem to kill it. Treatment with a systemic weedkiller in late summer, after first bruising the stems, will check the weed but will wipe out only isolated clumps.

HAIRY BITTERCRESS

This is the only annual in the garden weed directory, and it has been included for its remarkable success in colonising gardens. In nature, hairy bittercress (*Cardamine hirsuta*) grows in areas of open ground and has found the compost of container-grown plants very much to its liking, so many gardeners have unwittingly introduced the seeds that way. Hairy bittercress is also remarkable in being able to grow from seed to flower in a few weeks and to tolerate very cold weather so its numbers can build up very rapidly. The seeds are dispersed from spring-loaded seed pods just as you try to pull the plant up. To control hairy bittercress , hoe or handweed before it has flowered. Contact weedkillers can be used on unplanted land.

FIELD HORSETAIL

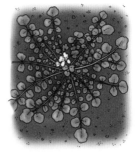

HAIRY BITTERCRESS

HELXINE

This delicate-looking plant, also known as baby's tears and mind-your-own-business (*Soleirolia soleirolii*), is used as an ornamental in glasshouses and rock gardens, but can become a problematic weed. It spreads rapidly on creeping stems that root as they go and thrive in damp, shady places. In a lawn, any cut section of stem can reroot, so helxine spreads quickly and it is not susceptible to any lawn weedkillers available to gardeners. To keep it in check, rake vigorously with a lawn rake in spring and autumn, and also feed the lawn. Alternatively, lift and replace sections of turf, or kill helxine using a systemic weedkiller (which will also kill the grass) then fork over and reseed. In a border, hoe helxine in dry weather, or smother it with mulch.

GROUND ELDER

Also known as bishop's weed or gout weed, ground elder (*Aegopodium podagraria*) is particularly troublesome in established plantings. Its fleshy, white, underground stems penetrate among other plants and if broken off soon regrow. Sometimes the only way to remove ground elder is to dig up the whole border in early autumn or spring, wash the roots of any wanted plants and pot these up or replant elsewhere. Dig the bed thoroughly; then allow any weed fragments to regrow until they can be dug out. When there is no more regrowth, replant the border. Alternatively, treat a border or area under a tree or shrub with a systemic weedkiller that is deactivated on soil contact. In uncultivated areas, use sheet mulches to smother these weeds.

HELXINE

GROUND ELDER

STINGING NETTLE

More than just a weed, stinging nettles (*Urtica dioica*) are invaluable wildlife plants; the stems contain fibres strong enough to make cloth, and the roots produce a yellow dye. Nevertheless, it's unwelcome in areas you want to cultivate, though its presence tends to indicate a fertile soil. Weaken stinging nettles by repeatedly cutting them, and put their shoots on the compost heap. With a little persistence, you can dig out their spreading stems, which root shallowly above and below the surface. Otherwise, spray with a systemic weedkiller before these weeds flower, taking care to protect wanted plants nearby until the weedkiller has dried. Small nettle is an annual, and easily controlled by hoeing.

PINK OXALIS

Another garden plant that has 'gone wrong' is pink oxalis (*Oxalis latifolia*), which is related to native wood sorrel. It has clover-like leaves and pretty, pink flowers, but in suitable conditions it can become very invasive. Tiny, dark-leaved, yellow oxalis (*O. corniculata*) can also be problematic. As well as seeds, both produce lots of small bulbils that readily separate from the parent and can live for years in the soil before growing when conditions are suitable. Dig plants out in spring, when the tubers are most firmly attached. Otherwise, apply a systemic weedkiller before flowering. Protect wanted plants in the vicinity until the weedkiller is dry. Even this treatment may have to be repeated for several years as more seeds and tubers grow.

STINGING NETTLE

PINK OXALIS

BROADLEAVED PLANTAIN

The tough foliage of broadleaved plantain (*Plantago major*) can lie very close to the ground, escaping the blades of the lawnmower and tolerating trampling. The leaves also shade out and kill nearby grass, giving the plantain room to grow. Although these weeds are well anchored with tough, fibrous roots, they can be levered out when the soil is moist, using a narrow trowel or daisy grubber. If numerous, treat broadleaved plantains with a liquid or granular lawn weedkiller, but for scattered rosettes a ready-to-use spray or spot treatment is preferable. Treat early in the year when the grass is growing vigorously and will quickly fill the spaces created by the death of these weeds.

FIELD WOODRUSH

Wiry, grass-like field woodrush (*Luzula campestris*) tends to thrive on light, acid soils where the grass is growing poorly. The leaves are broader and darker than grass, but it may go unnoticed until the brown flowers are produced in spring. Because it is closely related to grass, lawn weedkillers will not control field woodrush so the best approach to its eradication is a combination of hand pulling, together with liming to reduce soil acidity as well as feeding to improve the growth of lawn grasses. Take soil samples from areas where field woodrush is a problem and use a pH soil-testing kit to assess the pH of these samples. Then add lime to the soil until you have achieved a pH of 6.5–7.0.

183

BROADLEAVED PLANTAIN

FIELD WOODRUSH

LESSER YELLOW TREFOIL

One of a large number of clover-family lawn weeds, lesser yellow trefoil (*Trifolium dubium*) is an annual producing a mat of shoots anchored by tough roots and spreading mainly by seed. The mat-forming trefoils and medicks tend to smother the grass beneath them so show up quite prominently in lawns. More spreading clovers weave in between the grass, making them less conspicuous and less damaging. Weed out medicks and trefoils by tracing shoots back to the central root and cutting it below ground with a knife. Weaken spreading clovers by raking before mowing, to lift the stems so they are cut with the grass. These plants have limited susceptibility to lawn weedkillers.

HAWKWEEDS, DANDELIONS AND DAISIES

Hawkweeds, hawkbits, cat's ears, dandelions and daisies all belong to the same family and produce low-growing rosettes of leaves that enable them to survive in close-mown turf. Mouse-ear hawkweed (*Pilosella officinarum*) particularly favours light, dry soils, where the grass is weak, so it can form dense mats of leaves. Handweeding using a narrow trowel, hand fork or daisy grubber works for most of these weeds but beware the taproots of dandelions, which can regrow unless the whole root is removed. Treat individual weeds with ready-to-use sprays or other appropriate spot treatments. If weed growth is extensive, apply a liquid or granular lawn weedkiller, following the manufacturer's instructions.

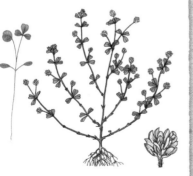

LESSER YELLOW TREFOIL

MOUSE-EAR HAWKWEED

SLENDER SPEEDWELL

Several speedwells can become lawn weeds including the pretty, blue-flowered germander speedwell. However slender speedwell (*Veronica filiformis*), originally introduced as a rock garden plant, is the most troublesome. It spreads with fine, creeping stems, which root as they extend. If cut, these stems readily develop into new plants, so mowing quickly spreads the problem. Slender speedwell is unaffected by weedkillers available to gardeners. Although vigorous raking with a lawn rake can remove much of the growth, slender speedwell will soon grow back, so it often has to be tolerated if it has spread over much of the lawn. The alternative is to use a systemic weedkiller, which will also kill the grass, then reseed.

YARROW

The feathery leaves of yarrow (*Achillea millefolium*) are not unattractive, and the dried flower stems have the distinction of being used for the Chinese I Ching system of divination. However, most gardeners would rather not have yarrow in their lawns, where it forms dense carpets of overlapping leaves, impervious to mowing. It spreads by low, branching stems, which root and grow even if severed from the parent. Dig out small patches or treat them with a ready-to-use spray or spot treatment. If scattered over a large area, apply a liquid or granular lawn weedkiller. Feed the surrounding grass to encourage vigorous growth, which should fill the gaps and outcompete any lingering yarrow shoots.

SLENDER SPEEDWELL

YARROW

• GLOSSARY •

Acid Soil with a low lime content, less than 7 on the pH scale.

Alkaline Soil with a high lime content, more than 7 on the pH scale.

Annual A plant that lives for less than a year.

Barrier glue A sticky substance used to trap insect pests that can't fly.

Bedding plant A flowering or foliage plant for temporary display outdoors.

Biennial A plant that completes its life cycle over two growing seasons, producing roots, stems and leaves in the first year, then flowering and setting seed in the second.

Biological control The use of one living organism to control another, usually a pest.

Brassica A member of the cabbage family.

Bulb Swollen, overlapping leaf bases that act as a food store and remain when the rest of the plant dies down: eg, an onion.

Chlorosis A deficiency of chlorophyll in green plants, in which leaves turn yellow; it is often caused by mineral deficiency.

Cloche A glass or plastic cover to protect plants from the weather.

Cold frame A wooden, metal or plastic framework, supporting glass or plastic panels, used to protect plants from extremes of weather.

Compost 1. Decayed plant material used as a soil improver or mulch. 2. A mix of materials used to grow plants in containers.

Conifer A tree or shrub that produces cones.

Contact [pesticide] A pesticide that has to make direct contact with the pest to be effective and is not absorbed by plant tissues.

Crop rotation A system of growing vegetables in order to control pests, diseases and fertility, so that the same crop is not grown continuously in the same soil.

Deciduous Used to describe a tree or shrub that loses its leaves over winter.

Ericaceous Literally 'heath-like' from *Erica*, the botanical name for heaths. Used to describe plants that, like some ericas, dislike lime.

Etiolated Pale and drawn; generally used of seedlings suffering from lack of light.

Evergreen Used to describe a tree, shrub or other perennial plant that does not lose its leaves over winter.

Family A plant group that is the next level up from a genus. Most families contain several genera: for example, the Liliaceae (lily family) includes lilies (*Lilium*) and tulips (*Tulipa*).

Fleece A thin, non-woven material, usually white, used to protect plants.

Fungicide A pesticide used to kill fungi, especially those that cause disease in plants.

Genus (plural, **genera**) A plant group that is the next level up from a species. The genus is always given as the first part of the botanical name. For example the regal lily, *Lilium regale*, is in the *Lilium* genus.

Germination The process by which a plant emerges from a seed.

Hardening off The process of gradually acclimatising plants raised in a warm, protected enviroment to outdoor conditions before planting out.

Herbaceous A non-woody plant.

Herbicide see Weedkiller.

Humus The dark substance in soil derived from organic material.

Insecticide A pesticide used to kill insects and, sometimes, other invertebrates such as mites.

Larva An immature insect: eg, a maggot or caterpillar.

Liquid feed A solution of fertiliser, which may be organic or inorganic.

Mulch A soil covering, which may be organic or inorganic, to limit water loss and reduce weeds.

Neutral Soil that is neither acid nor alkaline, ie, pH 7.

Organic material Technically, any material containing carbon, but normally used to mean material derived from living things.

Parasitic nematode A microscopic worm that lives as a parasite; often used to control pests by carrying pest-specific diseases.

Perennial A plant that lives for more than two years.

Pesticide Any substance used to control pests. May be a manufactured chemical, a naturally occurring mineral or a plant extract. Includes insecticides, fungicides, herbicides (weedkillers) and molluscicides (slug and snail killers)

Pheromone trap Pheromones are produced by female insects to attract males. The trap uses a manufactured copy to lure males to a sticky sheet.

pH A measure of acidity or alkalinity, from pH1 (the most acid) to pH14 (the most alkaline), used in gardening to refer to soils.

Pollinator An organism that transfers pollen from one flower to another. Birds, bats and insects are common pollinators.

187

Residual [weedkiller] A herbicide that breaks down slowly, so goes on controlling weeds over a period of several weeks.

Selective [herbicide] A weedkiller that kills some types of plant and not others: eg, lawn weedkillers kill broadleaved weeds but not grass.

Species A group of plants that share the same characteristics and can breed freely with each other.

Spot treatment Using an applicator (such as a wax stick) or a narrow spray jet, to treat individual weeds.

Sticky trap A method of controlling insects by catching them on a sticky sheet (such as fly paper).

Storage root A root that stores food, usually as starch, so the plant can survive difficult conditions: eg, winter cold, summer drought.

Systemic [pesticide] A pesticide that is absorbed by plants. Systemic insecticides can kill insects feeding on the plant without directly contacting them; systemic herbicides are carried down to a plant's roots.

Taproot A large main root that grows straight down into the ground. May become a food store: eg, a carrot.

Thinning The removal of some seedlings, flower buds, shoots or branches to reduce overcrowding and improve plant performance.

Tuber A swollen underground stem that acts as a food store and remains when the rest of the plant dies down: eg, a potato.

Variety A group of plants that vary in a consistent way from the basic species: eg, in flower colour.

Weedkiller (also known as **herbicide**) A chemical that kills plants (not just 'weeds').

· INDEX ·

189

• PICTURE CREDITS •

Note The acknowledgements below appear in source order.

....

Alamy Ian Shaw 36–7

Corbis Rolf Hicker 144–5

GAP Photos BIOS/Gilles Le Scanff & Joëlle-Caroline Mayer 129; Christa Brand 70; FhF Greenmedia 137; Fiona Lea 33 left, 66, 175 left; Fiona McLeod/design: Sean Swallow 116; Friedrich Strauss 38; Geoff Kid 35; Gerald Majumdar 10; John Glover 158; Leigh Clapp/ location Ringmer Park 100; Martin Hughes-Jones 175; Maxine Adcock 2, 29

Garden World Images Andrea Jones 8–9; Gary Smith 7; Dave Bevan 33 right, Georgianna Lane 50–1; Gilles Delacroix 54, 92; Jacqui Dracup 24; Liz Every 98; MAP/Arnaud Descat 85; Mark Bolton 105; Trevor Sims 175 centre

Photolibrary Garden Picture Library/Eric van Lokven 107; Garden Picture Library/ Stephen Shepherd 170–1

Thinkstock Hemera 52, 58, 148; iStockphoto 61, 63, 64, 76, 78, 82, 95, 108–9, 118, 159, 168